THE EVERYTHING® SIGN LANGUAGE BOOK
SECOND EDITION

Dear Reader,

As the parent of a son who was born profoundly deaf, I quickly realized how important it was for my son to communicate with those who were involved in his daily world. I also realized, after exploring a number of other methods, that signing was the most effective way for David to communicate. American Sign Language allowed him to express his needs and to share what was on his mind with other people. As I began my early journey into the world of sign language, instructional guides were limited. Books were difficult to understand and imitate, leaving many questions unanswered in acquiring this valuable mode of communication. Therefore, I've tried to make *The Everything® Sign Language Book, 2nd Edition* user-friendly, and it is my hope you will find this book offers an easy and pleasant learning journey into the wonderful world of sign language.

Over the past twenty-eight years, I have developed and taught courses and presented an array of in-services in American Sign Language and I have seen how enthusiasm and effort in learning this language can open doors and lead to improved communication for all. It has been a joy to watch students of all ages acquire a new way to communicate while they learn new things about themselves.

American Sign Language is a beautiful language that can communicate what is in your mind and in your heart. My wish for you is to learn from this book, enjoy what you learn, and, most importantly, use what you learn.

Sincerely,

Irene Duke

Welcome to the EVERYTHING® Series!

These handy, accessible books give you all you need to tackle a difficult project, gain a new hobby, comprehend a fascinating topic, prepare for an exam, or even brush up on something you learned back in school but have since forgotten.

You can choose to read an *Everything*® book from cover to cover or just pick out the information you want from our four useful boxes: e-questions, e-facts, e-alerts, and e-ssentials.

We give you everything you need to know on the subject, but throw in a lot of fun stuff along the way, too.

We now have more than 400 *Everything*® books in print, spanning such wide-ranging categories as weddings, pregnancy, cooking, music instruction, foreign language, crafts, pets, New Age, and so much more. When you're done reading them all, you can finally say you know *Everything*®!

E-QUESTION

Answers to
common questions

FACTS

Important snippets
of information

ALERTS!

Urgent
warnings

Quick
handy tips

PUBLISHER Karen Cooper

DIRECTOR OF ACQUISITIONS AND INNOVATION Paula Munier

MANAGING EDITOR, EVERYTHING SERIES Lisa Laing

COPY CHIEF Casey Ebert

ACQUISITIONS EDITOR Lisa Laing

SENIOR DEVELOPMENT EDITOR Brett Palana-Shanahan

EDITORIAL ASSISTANT Hillary Thompson

MODELS Molly Howitt and Tiffany Nardini

Visit the entire Everything® series at *www.everything.com*

THE
EVERYTHING®
SIGN
LANGUAGE
BOOK

SECOND EDITION

American Sign Language made easy

Irene Duke

Adams media
Avon, Massachusetts

This book is dedicated to my son David; to make his world a better place, and to my past, present and future students; and to the many others who will benefit from a better understanding of sign language.

An Everything® Series Book.
Everything® and everything.com® are registered trademarks of F+W Media, Inc.

Published by Adams Media, a division of F+W Media, Inc.
57 Littlefield Street, Avon, MA 02322 U.S.A.
www.adamsmedia.com

ISBN 10: 1-59869-883-4
ISBN 13: 978-1-59869-883-1

Printed in the United States of America.

10   9   8   7   6   5   4

Library of Congress Cataloging-in-Publication Data
is available from the publisher.

Interior photographs: Joe Ciarcia / Symphony Photography
Models: Molly Howitt and Tiffany Nardini

*This book is available at quantity discounts for bulk purchases.
For information, please call 1-800-289-0963.*

Contents

Top Ten Reasons You Should Learn Sign Language / x
Introduction / xi

1 What Is Sign Language? / 1
A Visual Form of Communication **2** • American Sign Language **2** • Signed English **3** • Contact Signing/Pidgin Sign English **4** • Home Signs **5** • Fingerspelling **5** • What You Will Learn **6** • Who Uses Sign Language? **8**

2 The Origins and History of Sign Language / 15
The Beginning **16** • The Creators **17** • The Golden Age of Deaf Education **19** • The Dark Age of Sign Language History **20** • A Year Worth Remembering **22** • Sign Language Today **23**

3 Strategies for Learning / 25
Early ASL Awkwardness **26** • Which Hand Do I Use? **26** • Some Signs Require Two Hands **27** • Strategies **30** • Eye Contact **31**

4 Fingerspelling / 33
Situations That Call for Fingerspelling **34** • Talking to Yourself **34** • Becoming an Accurate Fingerspeller **34** • Hand Warm-Up **36** • Spelling Bee **43** • Initialized Signs **44** • Fingerspelled Loan Signs **44** • Abbreviations and States **46**

5 Get a Firm Grip on the Rules / 49
The Big Four **50** • Signing Space **56** • Intonation **57** • Sign Etiquette **58** • Plurals **59** • Sign Order **60**

6 Questions, Questions! / 63

Two Types of Questions **64** • Applying Nonmanual Behaviors **64** • Answering Questions **66** • Signing Wh- Words **66** • Sign Variations **69** • The Interview **70** • Rhetorical Questions **76**

7 Variety Is the Spice of Life / 77

Describing People **78** • Color My World **78** • Dress Me Up **82** • They've Got the Look **85** • The Good and Bad **87** • Pronouns and Possessives **90**

8 Count 1-2-3 / 93

It's All in the Numbers **94** • Counting to Ten **94** • Conversations with Letters and Numbers **98** • Tackling Eleven Through Nineteen **98** • Counting to Ninety **100** • Big Numbers **102** • Fractions **103** • Money **104** • Signing Everyday Numbers **108**

9 Friends, Family, and Acquaintances / 109

Genders **110** • Family Relationships **110** • People You Know **114** • The Workplace and the ADA **117**

10 The Whole Picture / 119

A Face Is Worth a Thousand Signs **120** • Lean into It with Body Language **123** • Using Signs in Storytelling **124** • Classifiers, the Powerful Tool **127** • Mold It, Shape It **132**

11 Ready, Set, Go! / 135

Let Your Fingers Do the Walking **136** • Sport Signs **138** • Additional Compound Signs **140** • Play Ball! **141**

12 Father Time / 143

Past, Present, and Future **144** • Signing a Specific Time **146** • General Times **147** • Learning the Calendar **149** • Time to Celebrate **153**

13 The Great Outdoors / 157

A Word about Service Dogs **158** • The Menagerie **160** • The Weatherman **167** • Nature's Best **170**

14 Let the Banquet Begin / 173

Don't Skip Breakfast **174** • Lunchtime! **176** • Afternoon Snack **180** • The Evening Meal **181** • Sweet Temptations **185**

15 Around and About / 189

Home Sweet Home **190** • The Telephone and the TTY **192** • Computers **194** • School Days **198** • Working Nine to Five **203**

16 What's Up, Doc? / 207

In Sickness and in Health **208** • The "Broken Ear" **211** • First Aid **212** • Exploring the Ear **217** • Caution: Fragile Ear! **219** • Cochlear Implants **223**

17 Around the World / 225

Sign Variations **226** • On the Road Again **227** • The Three-Finger Classifier **232** • Location and Direction **234** • Time for a Vacation **234**

18 New Age of Sign Language / 239

Baby Talk **240** • Sign Language and Early Education **242** • Hearing Health **245** • Simplified Signs **246** • Many Faces of Sign **247**

19 **Expressing Yourself with Signing / 249**

Signing Music **250** • Visual Tapestries Within the Arts **253** • Developing Expressions and Body Language **254** • The Art of Drama **255**

20 **Further Your Skills / 257**

Everyday Chatter **258** • Using Games to Learn **259** • Total Communication **262** • Cued Speech **263** • A Quick Pop Quiz **263** • Variety of Communication **264**

Appendix A: Quizzes and Games / 265

Alphabet Quiz **265**; True/False Awareness Quiz **266**; Letter Form Quiz **267**; Sign Practice Quiz **268**; Quiz Answers **270**; Sign Language Games **271**

Appendix B: Resources / 275

Deaf/Sign Language Resources **275**; Websites **277**; Sign Language Books **278**; Videos and CDs **281**

Appendix C: Glossary / 282

Index / 287

ACKNOWLEDGMENTS

I wish to express my appreciation to the wonderful staff of Massasoit College for their encouragement and support in writing the second edition of *The Everything® Sign Language Book*. In addition, my thanks to my kind friends, Genie and the staff of Whitman Hanson Regional School District, who provided me with the faith that the first edition would actually become a reality. I send forth sincere gratitude to my mentor, Beth, for the many years she provided me with guidelines to writing and for her friendship. My sincerest gratitude to all of my past and present students from Massasoit College, the vast number of Early Educators, the caring parents, and the countless participants of the American Sign Language (ASL) courses, in-services, and workshops. These students and participants have provided me with endless resources to write a more concise second edition. My greatest appreciation is given to my friend and sister who, once again, burned the midnight oil with me, held my hand, and spent hours every weekend typing. Finally, I am sending my eternal, loving appreciation to my husband for his endless support and his constant unconditional love.

Top Ten Reasons
You Should Learn Sign Language

1. To be able to communicate effectively with the Deaf and hard of hearing.

2. To have fun learning a new and exciting visual language.

3. To look great on a resume and to open doors for new employment opportunities.

4. To spur intellectual growth and raise IQ.

5. To open new avenues for friendships and relationships.

6. To improve self-confidence and enhance communication skills.

7. To experience another avenue for expressing yourself artistically.

8. To broaden language acquisition in the early classroom.

9. To acquire the skill of nonverbal communication, body language, and facial expressions.

10. To learn a new language that can satisfy high school or college modern and foreign language requirements.

Introduction

▶ IT'S OBVIOUS THAT you're interested in sign language; otherwise you wouldn't have picked up this book. But did you know that you already use a natural form of gestural language every day? Nodding your head "yes," shaking your head "no," telling someone to call by holding an imaginary phone to your ear, and saying hello with a friendly wave are all natural gestures. With your natural gestures and this book in hand, you have already given yourself a wonderful head start into learning the basics of sign language.

This sign language book is user-friendly. It is designed to acclimate you slowly into the various parts of sign language, while being fun at the same time. It is not meant to be a heavy textbook or a sign language dictionary. It is concise in detail and filled with fantastic sign images using real models. Each chapter offers an easy and cumulative learning experience, and signs are presented in a progressive pattern.

While this book can be used on its own, it can also be used in conjunction with an American Sign Language (ASL) course and to assist in natural language acquisition through interaction with deaf friends, relatives, and their community. This book serves as a friendly bridge between the classroom, sign dictionary, and text. It will also fill in the gray areas those new signers often find confusing or challenging. You will acquire a better understanding of the various applications for sign language and the population that uses this visual mode of communication.

Perhaps you are a person who has studied languages but never received any real gratification—and certainly not instant gratification—from those studies. American Sign Language is different from other languages in that if you follow the easy-to-read instructions, you will be able to form signs quickly. The basic signs are easy to learn, and before you know it, you will be stringing them together in short sentences. This is true even if you are a person whose life is constantly punctuated by interruptions—you will be able pick up this book, put it down at your leisure, and still learn!

You can share the learning experience with family and friends by having them watch while you form the signs and see if you are signing it the way the images appear in the book. You can encourage them to learn with you and try to hold conversations using simple signs and natural gestural signs. Parents of young children can practice the basic signs while reading to their children, thus enhancing story time and language. At the same time, parents will be giving their children a head start in their own acquisition of ASL at the time when their language acquisition skills are most keen. A trip to a zoo, aquarium, or museum can be made into an exciting visually interactive language experience with the use of signs for the entire family.

You will be able to teach others the letters of the alphabet and practice fingerspelling words—this, of course, is after you have learned to sign all the letters of the manual alphabet. Some of the basic signs that are introduced here could be just enough for you to provide a patient in a hospital some comfort until an interpreter arrives. Then again, this book may spark enough interest to get you to consider changing your college focus or your career or motivate you to seek out that special job that requires communicating with a diverse population. Regardless of whether you have the opportunity to use sign language with a deaf or hard-of-hearing person, you will still be enriched by learning American Sign Language.

CHAPTER 1

What Is Sign Language?

Sign language is a complete visual mode of communication. It is the third most-used language in the United States and the fourth most-used language worldwide. Conversations and information, using sign language, are conveyed visually rather than auditorily and are composed of precise handshapes and movements. Sign language users combine articulate hand movements, facial expressions, head and body movements to communicate feelings, intentions, humor, complex and abstract ideas, and more. There is a great deal to learn about this language, its types, and its users, and this chapter will help introduce you to this unique and astonishing language.

A Visual Form of Communication

Most languages are based on audible sounds. People are naturally accustomed to language that is spoken, and for many people, daily communication is received and understood through hearing. However, sign language is a *visually* based form of communication that is received and understood through our powers of vision. Simply stated, it is listening with your eyes.

In the signing world, it is important to know and recognize the primary types of sign language. Therefore, before going any further, you should concentrate on learning about a few of the different types of sign language. While there are several, the next sections will focus on the five most commonly known types: American Sign Language, Signed English, Contact Signing/Pidgin Sign English, Home Signs, and Fingerspelling.

American Sign Language

American Sign Language, known as ASL, is the natural native language of the American Deaf community. ASL is used as the primary form of communication in the daily lives of the Deaf. Even so, a portion of the Deaf population does not use ASL. The reasons for this can range from personal choice to parental influences, educational philosophies, or regional and geographical locations.

Often, people are under the misconception that ASL is just a form of manual English. On the contrary, ASL is a separate living, natural language that has developed over the years within the Deaf community. ASL is a full language with its own syntax, punctuations, and grammar. American Sign Language is composed of precise handshapes, palm positions, movements, and the use of space around the signer.

E-QUESTION

Why is a capital "D" used in the word Deaf?
It is used to create a distinction. The lowercase word "deaf" refers to the physical condition of hearing loss. The uppercase word "Deaf" refers to the Deaf community, which shares a common language, cultural heritage, and similar interests.

These elements, movements, and handshapes, supported by facial expressions and body language, are capable of conveying complex and abstract ideas as well as humor, wit, and poetry. ASL is constantly evolving and often changes regionally. In addition, ASL also counts as a language credit at various colleges, universities, and high schools throughout the country. The following combined elements serve to make ASL an exciting, effective form of communication:

- ASL signs
- Limited fingerspelling
- Facial expressions
- Body language
- Head movement
- Use of space and directional movement

Signed English

Signed English, known as SE, is a complete visual presentation of English. In this system, one word is equal to one sign, and the signs are presented in English word order. Additional signing time is required when using SE, due to the many add-on elements needed for each signed word. These elements can consist of prefixes, suffixes, endings, and tenses. Because of the English components, SE is used in various educational settings. The focus in this type of sign application is to enhance and promote English and its grammar while building reading and writing skills. SE can be found in legal situations or in a court of law where it is legally imperative to demonstrate every word. This form of signing has also been adopted by hearing parents of deaf children who may feel more comfortable with the strong English order. English-speaking adults who have lost their hearing often lean toward Signed English.

Here are some of the elements that comprise SE:

- Standard signs
- Fingerspelling
- Initialization (see Chapter 4)

- Prefixes
- Suffixes
- Endings
- One word equals one sign
- English word order

Contact Signing/Pidgin Sign English

Contact Signing, also known as PSE (Pidgin Sign English), is a sign system that uses ASL signs in approximate English word order, omitting prefixes, suffixes, endings, and small words. It is important for you to be aware that the term Pidgin Sign English is greatly falling out of favor with the Deaf community. Today, the term Contact Signing is preferred over PSE. Contact Signing is often used to help bridge the communication gap between the deaf, the Deaf community, and the hearing. This is especially true in situations where a signer has limited ASL skills. Contact Signing is a sign system that allows signers to manage a limited signed conversation.

Perhaps it is best to describe the Contact Signing system as a cross between English and ASL. Often it is used as a transitional step in the process of acclimating someone into ASL. Depending on the skills of the signer, this system can vary in degrees between English and ASL.

FACT

Total Communication, referred to as TC, uses all means available for communication: sign language, gesturing, lip reading, fingerspelling, speech, hearing aids, reading, writing, and visual images.

Contact Signing is used by a number of educators, employers, and service providers quite successfully. Often, hearing parents of deaf children and students new to the study of ASL use Contact Signing in their early learning stages. In addition, a percentage of late-deafened adults adopt Contact Signing as a support method of communication. They have expressed a sense of comfort with the approximate English order of ASL signs. This is quite natural, as English is their first language. Parents of children who have had cochlear implants are also, in the formative years of language development, adopting Contact Signing.

Characteristics of Contact Signing include the following:

- Standard signs
- ASL signs
- Fingerspelling
- Facial expressions
- Body language
- Approximate English word order

Home Signs

Home signs are invented signs that are combined with some standard ASL or SE signs, pantomime, and natural gestures. Home signs are invented primarily out of necessity. This type of signing occurs when sign language or a specific sign for a word is not known. This inventive approach to language is a normal progression. It often occurs with young children and in situational groups.

During the course of your life, perhaps without realizing it, you create special words for family, workplaces, and things. These affectionate names are then only recognized within your close circles of friends, coworkers, and family members. Home signs function in much the same way. It would not be unusual to see a young Deaf child, not knowing the proper signs for nouns, signing "brown balls" to represent a cocoa-flavored cereal or "purple drink" for grape juice. So as you become more aware of the different types of sign language, be on the lookout for home signs that use descriptive adjectives rather than properly signed names and nouns.

Fingerspelling

Fingerspelling is a way of representing a word by spelling it out, letter by letter. It uses the American Manual Alphabet, which is a set of separate handshapes representing each of the twenty-six letters of the English alphabet. Watching and reading every letter of each word can be exhausting, and you will need to keep this in mind. ASL uses limited fingerspelling. However, fingerspelling and the handshapes of the manual alphabet do play important roles in signing. You will get a better understanding of this technique in Chapter 4.

What You Will Learn

Now that you have a major portion of the technical information behind you, try your hand at a pop quiz. Without looking back, can you remember what these acronyms represent?

- ASL
- SE
- PSE

If you answered American Sign Language, Signed English, and Pidgin Sign English, good for you! It is important to remember these three acronyms. Once you venture into the signing world, you will find that they are used repeatedly in discussions of types of sign language. It is quite common to be asked what type of signing you know and use and where you acquired your skill. As you move forward in this book, you will see the acronym ASL used throughout, as this type of sign language will be the primary focus of this book. The term "sign language" will be used only as a generic form.

E-QUESTION

How many colleges and universities in the United States offer sign language as a foreign, modern, or world language?
The numbers of colleges and universities that accept and offer American Sign Language for academic credit grows each year. At this time, approximately 180 four-year colleges and universities accept ASL to satisfy the foreign and modern language requirement. Over 600 colleges and universities around the country offer ASL in their curriculum. Public schools, K-12, have also begun to recognize ASL as a world language.

Sign Vocabulary

You will soon acquire, through visual sign images and accompanying instructions, a broad basic sign vocabulary. Add just a little daily practice and a smidgen of determination and you will be well on your way to reaching the Level I of basic ASL. To make your learning journey more interesting and easy to comprehend, the book contains hundreds of detailed sign images. The visual journey begins by understanding the detailed images you will be viewing throughout the book. Please note that all of the images are displayed with the model facing you, the receiver/reader. In other words, simply think that someone is directly signing to you. Also, most images demonstrated throughout this book show a right-handed signer.

Just take a close look at these two images, which illustrate the signs for "hello" and "sign." These two signs are a great beginning and among the most often used signs.

▲ **HELLO:** The starting position of the hand is similar to a military salute. Then, simply wave your hand off your forehead.

▲ **SIGN:** Position both hands in front of the chest with both index fingers extended, and palms facing each other. Circle your hands, alternately rotating them toward your body.

Signs and Rules

Soon, you will learn the basic rules for fingerspelling, sign order, facial expression, and body language. In addition, you will learn strategies to make learning sign language easy and fun. You will also acquire knowledge of the particular framework that sets sign language apart from spoken languages.

There are also rules regarding signing etiquette and rules regarding the American Disabilities Act that will be presented. Moreover, there are important dos and don'ts to learn regarding the deaf, the Deaf community, and the hard of hearing in medical situations. Of course, there will be many little tidbits of information to enjoy and to build on.

Who Uses Sign Language?

First and foremost, sign language is used in the Deaf community, by the hard of hearing, the deaf/blind, and interpreters for the deaf. In addition, it is used by parents, family, friends, and service providers for the deaf and the Deaf community, who support the use of signing as a way to communicate.

The use of sign language has also expanded into many various settings that are not related to the deaf population. An example of this is the application of sign language in educational settings. Educational applications can range from enhancement of language in young children to assisting communication within the highly diverse special-needs population. (However, it must be noted that the use of this type of basic sign language does not and cannot compare to the pure ASL used within the Deaf community.)

An interpreter is a person who facilitates communication for the deaf, the hard of hearing, and hearing persons by translating spoken language into sign language.

Whatever your reasons are for learning and using sign language, the result will be a positive experience and an additional life skill. Perhaps you will find your occupation or special interest mentioned in the sections that follow. Perhaps you are simply fascinated with this visual language. Following is a look at the occupations and special interests that often require skill in sign language.

Special-Needs Educators

Special-needs educators apply visual signs to stimulate, ease, and assist communication. Within the challenged population, the signs adopted for use are often modified or simplified. Using modified signs accommodates the diverse challenges of special-needs children and adults alike. Each year, the number of special-needs educators who adopt visual signs for use within a classroom setting increases. Special-needs job trainers and various service providers who are involved with independent living programs are also using signs as a means of supporting communication and providing information.

Regular Educators

As each year passes, more educators in high schools and colleges support the acceptance of ASL as a second language. Courses in American Sign Language are now being taught for academic credit in world, foreign, and modern language programs.

FACT

In 1989, the U.S. Supreme Court recognized American Sign Language as a standard independent language with its own grammar, syntax, vocabulary, and cultural heritage. This court ruled that ASL could be offered in all public and secondary schools to satisfy foreign language requirements.

Educators working within regular educational systems are witnessing the enrichment that ASL brings to the lives of their students. Today, you will see ASL students in upper grades of high schools go into the lower grades and share their knowledge. They stage fun-filled demonstrations in sign language to the delight of the younger students. You will also find college students applying their signing skills in community service projects, in school programs for children, in their places of worship, on their jobs, and in the practicum. These students often become the greatly needed interpreters or service providers for the deaf, the Deaf community, and the hard of hearing.

This refreshing new fascination with ASL as a second language has piqued the interest of teachers and paraprofessionals. School systems are now starting to offer basic ASL courses for their staff as well. The goal is to bring this language into the classroom to enhance language and communication skills. As a result, teachers and support staff are also reaping the benefits that come from the acceptance of ASL as a second language in educational systems.

Children of Deaf Adults

Today, there is a higher probability that students whose parents are deaf will be enrolling into a public school system. These students are known as "CODAs" within the Deaf community. CODA, or Children of Deaf Adults, are bilingual and bicultural as a result of the Deaf environment in which they grow up. Yet at the same time, these children also live, socialize, and attend schools in the hearing world. The acronym KODA, or Kids of Deaf Adults, represents the younger portion of this population.

FACT

The Americans with Disabilities Act is a federal civil rights law protecting individuals with disabilities. It guarantees individuals with disabilities equal opportunity and access to state and local government services, public accommodations, employment, transportation, communication and telecommunications.

The use of sign language in this type of situation would have a double purpose. First, ASL would likely be the primary method of communication for members of the Deaf community who are parents. Therefore, signing would be required for effective communication between the parents and school personnel. Deaf parents are generally pleased to learn that a school has staff members who can sign, even if their signing skills are basic. Basic signing skills can serve as a bridge until an interpreter arrives for meetings or teacher conferences. These simple signing skills can also provide helpful information in the event there is an emergency involving the child. It is important to remember that the Americans with Disabilities Act, or ADA, mandates that an interpreter be provided to ensure that deaf parents receive equal access to communication.

The second application of sign language would be for the ease and comfort of the KODA student into a classroom setting. In all probability, ASL will be the student's first language. Signing, to some degree, may be necessary to support spoken language and facilitate the first year of school for the young bilingual student of Deaf parents.

Early Educators and Providers

Early educators and providers are using sign language to enhance language acquisition and build cognitive skills. Through the efforts of these educators and providers, young children are able to experience the fun that comes from learning signed vocabulary. Excitement fills the air as young children learn signs through a variety of games, signed stories, and singing and signing songs. At the same time, these providers are also instilling children with an awareness and sensitivity toward children who have verbal, mental, and physical challenges. They are able to teach children that signing is simply another way of communicating and that it is okay to be different.

Public Employees

Police officers, firefighters, and first responders have also gained an interest in sign language. Many have completed courses in ASL or are presently enrolled in a program of ASL studies. This, in turn, is improving access to communication for the deaf, the Deaf community and the hard of hearing when the need arises for services provided by public employees. In addition, this interest has benefited all involved by promoting positive attitudes and awareness toward the deaf.

Medical Personnel

Medical professionals, such as doctors, nurses, emergency medical technicians, paramedics, hospital staff, medical centers, and physicians' offices are quickly realizing the advantages of knowing basic sign language. In the medical community, it is becoming more common for doctors, hospitals, and medical centers to be visited by deaf adults.

A very large percentage of these deaf adults are part of what is known as the "Rubella Bulge" of the 1960s. Also called the German Measles Epidemic, the Rubella Bulge created an enormous surge in incidences of deafness. Of those pregnant women who contracted German measles, or rubella, an extraordinarily high number had infants who were born with birth defects. These defects ranged from deafness, heart conditions, and blindness to complicated multiple birth defects. Between 1963 and 1965 alone, over 30,000 Rubella babies were born. The estimated rate of hearing loss was 73 percent.

ESSENTIAL

Sign language interpreters who are trained in medical signs should always be used when a deaf patient is unable to comfortably communicate or comprehend information. In addition, interpreters must be provided when medical diagnoses, treatment, and information is complex, according to the ADA.

Today, this portion of the Deaf population ranges in age from the mid-thirties to early fifties. They are now starting to experience their share of medical concerns and problems. Members of various medical communities are learning basic signs. The goal is to help ease frustrations experienced by deaf patients in communicating some of their basic medical needs.

Presently, sign language classes boast a high enrollment of medical personnel. If the medical profession is your interest or future line of work, you will be pleased to know that in this book there is an entire chapter dedicated to the medical field. (See Chapter 16.)

Service Providers

Service providers working in the following areas are exposed daily to a large percentage of the public. The probability of encountering a deaf or hard-of-hearing person who is seeking services from any of these areas increases with every passing year:

- Federal, state, and town agencies
- Postal services, banks, transportation
- Restaurants, retailers, hotels, theaters
- Libraries, parks, museums
- Ministries, churches, synagogues

The enormous increase in the deafened population that resulted from the German Measles Epidemic has and will have far-reaching effects on service providers. Today, the population of the Rubella Bulge is thriving. They are now adults and are members of Deaf communities, who have spread out all across the country. Many are married, have children, pay taxes, own cars, and support homes. They live their daily lives no differently than the average American. This also means they are consumers of products and services in all areas. The chances of anyone meeting, providing services to, or employing members of this Deaf community continuously increase.

CHAPTER 2

The Origins and History of Sign Language

The early evolution of sign language—that is, before the eighteenth century—remains unclear. However, there have been significant documented events and contributions to this ever-changing, living language. In this chapter, you will stroll through a few of the interesting pathways that have led to the development of sign language in America.

The Beginning

Try to imagine language in prehistoric times. It is easy to visualize a gestural sign language that members of a tribe might have used among themselves on a hunt. For instance, these hunters might have gestured to one another to maintain silence while hunting their wild game. Now move forward in time and imagine how languages crossed and mixed as the human population spread across the continents. As one language met a new, strange tongue, it is very probable that natural, gestural signing would have occurred while people figured out how to bridge their language gaps.

A Native System of Sign Language

People from the earliest times to the present have always communicated to some degree using their hands. Therefore, long before the documented events of the nineteenth century, it can be surmised that a native system of sign language existed among deaf people. In all probability, this deaf population would have used regional, geographical, or indigenous sign systems. They also would have created their own signs, such as the home signs discussed in Chapter 1. There is an interesting American historical record describing such an example between the seventeenth and nineteenth centuries on Martha's Vineyard in Massachusetts.

Vineyard Sign Language

An example of an indigenous sign language community existed on Martha's Vineyard, an island off the coast of Cape Cod, Massachusetts. It was here, from the late 1600s through the early 1900s, that the hearing population and the Deaf community developed and used its own sign language system. An extraordinarily high rate of genetic deafness on the island perpetuated the use of the Vineyard Sign Language, as it is called. Due to intermarriage among the islanders, this high rate of genetic deafness continued for 200 years.

Nonetheless, this community flourished, with hearing and Deaf islanders working and signing side by side. Vineyard Sign Language was handed down from generation to generation through the native signers. With the arrival of deaf education on the mainland, the lives of the population began to change. Deaf children attended new residential schools on the mainland, bringing with them their native sign language.

FACT

According to census reports, deafness in the American population during the nineteenth century occurred in 1 person out of every 6,000. The rate for deafness on Martha's Vineyard, however, was 1 in 155.

On the mainland, these children eventually found spouses, married, and settled down to live. Thus began the gradual decline in the numbers of the Deaf islanders on Martha's Vineyard. But, at the same time, Vineyard signs added to and merged with ASL signs on the mainland.

The Creators

It was during the eighteenth century that sign language began to take a recorded shape in history. Beginning in France in the 1700s, Abbé Charles Michel de l'Epee opened the first free school that served as a shelter for the deaf. The school supplied food, housing, and most importantly, education. Abbé de l'Epee studied and mastered the natural French signs of the deaf, called Old French Sign Language (OFSL). However, he believed these French signs were lacking in grammar.

Abbé Charles Michel de l'Epee

Abbé de l'Epee, being creative and with charitable intentions, modified the grammar of these signs. This resulted in a methodical signed version of spoken French called Old Sign French (OSF). What l'Epee perhaps failed to realize was that, in all probability, OFSL had its own grammar, just as ASL has its own grammar. The impact of l'Epee's grammar modifications was later debated with regard to sign language in America.

Later, Abbé de l'Epee trained Abbé Roch Sicard in Old Sign French. Sicard became a teacher of the deaf and a school director. A significant contribution to sign language was made by Abbé Sicard in 1782, with his writing of an elaborate dictionary of signs, *Theory of Signs*.

FACT

During the French Revolution, Abbé Roch Sicard was imprisoned and nearly executed. He spent two years in hiding, and it was during this time he wrote his dictionary of signs.

Thomas Gallaudet

Thomas Gallaudet, an American Congregational minister, met Abbé Sicard in 1816 while in search of methods to educate deaf children. He also met a deaf man by the name of Laurent Clerc. Clerc was Sicard's protégé and chief assistant and was considered a master teacher. So impressed was Gallaudet with Clerc—who was fluent in OSF, OFSL, and French—that he invited him to America to establish the first school for the deaf.

In 1816, Clerc and Gallaudet set sail on a fifty-five-day voyage to America. During this time, Clerc taught Gallaudet Old Sign French, and Gallaudet tutored Clerc in English. On April 15, 1817, they opened the first school for the deaf. The school was located in Connecticut, and had seven students enrolled. Gallaudet served as principal and Clerc the head teacher.

E-QUESTION

What is CODA?
CODA is the acronym meaning "Children of Deaf Adults." Today, CODA is a nonprofit organization for the hearing sons and daughters of deaf parents. The organization began in 1983 and presently includes people from many different countries. Further information on this subject can be found in Chapter 1.

Gallaudet advocated and lectured for the education of the deaf. He married deaf alumna Sophia Fowler and started a large family of CODAs. Gallaudet retired from the Hartford school in 1830 and devoted his time to his ministries and writings supporting deaf education and sign language. He also devoted time to writing children's books. He died in 1851, at the age of sixty-four, leaving behind a remarkable legacy in deaf education.

Laurent Clerc

Laurent Clerc taught and advocated for the deaf in America for forty-one years. During that time, he trained future hearing and deaf teachers. These future teachers spread out across America, teaching and establishing schools using Clerc's teaching methods.

The first established school for the deaf was called the Connecticut Asylum at Hartford for the Instruction of Deaf and Dumb Persons. Today, this school is known as The American School for the Deaf, with more than 4,000 alumni over its long history.

In 1818, Laurent Clerc successfully went before the U.S. Congress to gain support for deaf education. He was the first deaf person to address Congress. Thirty residential schools were established during Clerc's lifetime, a credit to his great influence on deaf education of that period. Clerc's Old Sign French blended with the modified and indigenous signs of the students. Today, it is believed that this melding eventually evolved into what is now known as American Sign Language.

The Golden Age of Deaf Education

Between the years 1818 and 1912, more than thirty schools for the deaf were established. These schools were established by deaf teachers, hearing teachers, and deaf students who were alumni of the American School for the Deaf and Gallaudet College.

Gallaudet College was established in Washington, D.C., in 1864. It was and still remains the only liberal arts college exclusively for the deaf, both in the United States and in the world. Originally, the college was named the

Columbia Institution for the Instruction of the Deaf and Dumb and the Blind. By the request of the alumni, in 1893, the name of the college was changed to honor Thomas Hopkins Gallaudet. Gallaudet's son, Edward Miner Gallaudet, became the first president of Gallaudet College. Today Gallaudet is a bustling campus with approximately 1,680 students. The campus continues to expand, offering a vast array of programs and new research centers. Gallaudet University now boasts 15,000 alumni, nationally and internationally.

Here are some little-known involvements between the Gallaudet College and United States presidents. Abraham Lincoln signed an act of Congress establishing accreditation for Gallaudet College and was its first patron. Ronald Reagan accorded university status to Gallaudet College in 1986. And in a tradition that began with Ulysses S. Grant in 1869, the president of the United States, as patron of the university, signs all diplomas.

Between the years 1840 and 1912, American Sign Language flourished across the United States. These years were known as the Golden Age of Deaf Education, and approximately 40 percent of all the deaf educators were deaf themselves. Sadly, this golden age went into a downslide near the end of the nineteenth century.

The Dark Age of Sign Language History

In 1880, the Milan Congress on Education for the Deaf voted to abolish the use of sign language in deaf education. Instead, oralism was adopted as the preferred method in deaf education worldwide. Oralism was a technique used in educating the deaf that relied solely on lip-reading, speech, and auditory training, instead of using signs. As the oralism method in deaf education began to take hold, it brought about what can be called the Dark Age of Deaf History.

Institutions that used sign language were reformed, and hundreds of oral schools were opened. Some states adopted laws prohibiting the use of signing in public schools. Deaf students were punished and reprimanded. One of the forms of punishment was the wearing of white mittens. These mittens had a short string attaching the hands together limiting the student's ability to sign. Deaf teachers across the country lost their positions during this transition into oralism. However, children in oral schools clandestinely signed in dorms and play areas. It was with tenacity that ASL survived this suppression.

FACT

The oralist approach became deeply rooted in the state of Massachusetts. In 1867, the Clarke School in Northampton was established, becoming the first truly oral school for the deaf.

Manualism Versus Oralism

The great debate between proponents of manualism (signing) and supporters of oralism raged on, and after 200 years, some differences still separate the parties. This was evidenced in 1995 when Miss Alabama, Heather Whitestone, who is deaf, won the coveted title of Miss America. Whitestone was criticized for choosing to speak rather than use sign language. Again, the debate was sparked, and it received front-page attention within the Deaf community.

Is Sign Language Really a "Language"?

Another debate raged over the question of whether sign language was a true language or a string of simple gestures. Dr. William C. Stokoe Jr., known as the father of ASL, proved in 1960 that American Sign Language meets all the requisite linguistic criteria to be classified as a fully developed language.

His research work and the books he published brought about the acceptance of ASL as an appropriate language of instruction for the deaf, in addition to its status as an appropriate second language for hearing students in higher education. Dr. Stokoe was a tireless advocate for the linguistic and educational rights of the Deaf, and he continued to actively write and publish until his death in 2000.

How many different forms of sign language are in existence?
Presently, worldwide there are at least 200 different forms of sign language in existence. Just as spoken languages vary, sign language also varies throughout the world. Even within the United States, there are regional differences; therefore, there are sign variations from state to state.

A Year Worth Remembering

In 1988, a new and respected heroine made her entrance into the chapters of sign language and Deaf history. Deaf actress Marlee Matlin captured the Oscar for Best Actress in her role in *Children of a Lesser God*. Matlin, who uses sign language, continues to work in many acting roles, such as those she has played in the television series *The West Wing*, *Picket Fences*, *Reasonable Doubts*, *My Name is Earl*, and *The L Word*. To date, Marlee has appeared in all kinds of roles in movies and television programs, *CSI: NY*, *Hollywood Squares*, *Law & Order*, *Extreme Makeover: Home Edition*, *Sweet Nothing in My Ear*, and *Dancing with the Stars*. Marlee has written three books that are loosely based on her own experiences growing up deaf in Chicago. Much is owed to Marlee Matlin, who with her fame, brings about awareness and exposure to the use of sign language. At the same time, Marlee continues to break the stereotyping of deaf people and strives to open the door for other deaf actors.

At the same time, in 1988, an extraordinary and significant event took place in the annals of Deaf history. Students at Gallaudet University in Washington, D.C., staged a weeklong protest and brought national attention to their revolutionary demand for a "Deaf President Now." Gallaudet students forced the closure of the campus with their demand for the appointment of a Deaf university president. The revolt was sparked when Elizabeth Ann Zinser, the only hearing candidate of a field of three finalists, was voted president. Zinser had relatively little experience with ASL or the Deaf population. Support grew throughout the week for the issue and the protesting students' agenda. These were their four demands:

1. Appointment of a Deaf president
2. Resignation of chairwoman Jane Spillman, who spoke unfavorably of the Deaf
3. The board of trustees would be comprised of Deaf members, representing 51 percent
4. No repercussions for those involved in the protest

On Friday, March 11, 1988, 3,000 protesters marched to the U.S. Capitol building with their demands. By Sunday, all their demands had been met, and Dr. I. King Jordan was appointed the first Deaf president of Gallaudet University. This victory was an exceptional turning point for members of the Deaf community, their culture, identity, and their beloved language. On October 16, 2006, another protest was held at Gallaudet University in Washington, D.C. The protest was over the appointment of Jane K. Fernandes as the next president of the school for the deaf.

It is important to remember that one cannot separate sign language history from the history of the Deaf community. Pure ASL belongs to the Deaf community with its rich and tenacious history. Throughout the remaining chapters, you will find informational pieces on the Deaf community, and its culture. In addition, you will find resources for further studies on this subject in Appendix B.

Sign Language Today

Today, ASL is thriving and is the fourth most studied language on campuses. Sign language has held its value and place in deaf education. Parents of deaf children have multiple choices in education. The Deaf community and its culture are holding fast with their consistent tenacity. The deaf population who were part of the 1960s rubella epidemic are active adults and contributing to the everyday economy. All of this brings us right back to the points discussed in Chapter 1, namely, the need in society today for people who are familiar with sign language. History has shown there will always be a need for the use of sign language. ASL will, therefore, remain a thriving, constantly evolving language. In addition, it will always be a language that enriches the lives of all those who become involved with its use.

CHAPTER 3

Strategies for Learning

This book will help you learn sign language slowly and steadily, moving through one chapter at a time. Each chapter acts as a building block. In this chapter, you will learn which is your dominant signing hand, gain valuable learning strategies, and get to know some rules and elements of ASL. Push up your sleeves, and get ready to work!

Early ASL Awkwardness

Don't be afraid of making errors. Remember: To err is human. Everyone makes mistakes. It's really no big deal if you make an error while learning ASL. It's all just part of the learning process and has no serious consequences. Your mistakes might even produce a few laughs! Silly signing errors happen consistently in Level I ASL classes. Just have a good giggle, move on, and learn from your errors.

Whatever you do, don't get discouraged. Don't give up. You *can* learn ASL, and have fun while you are learning. Although there are no shortcuts to learning how to form each sign, there is plenty of support in these pages. With a little determination, a positive attitude, and a dab of courage, you'll be signing with confidence in no time.

Those new to ASL often express frustration and discomfort during the first few weeks of learning. Have patience until you get past this awkward stage. You may experience these feelings:

- You are not in control of your arms and hands.
- You have no idea why your hands formed a particular sign.
- What you have signed is not what you intended.

These are all normal feelings. They will all soon dissipate, and then you can look back and smile about your early ASL awkwardness. Be patient. This is a new and different way of communicating, and acclimating to a visual language takes time. Just dig in your heels, and go to it.

Which Hand Do I Use?

This is the most commonly asked question, and it is quite easy to answer. You will use your stronger and naturally dominant hand. This hand is the one you use daily while writing, eating, turning a screwdriver, and doing most tasks. Therefore, if you are right-handed, then your right hand will be your dominant signing hand. If you use your left hand for most daily tasks, then the left becomes your dominant signing hand. For those novice signers who are ambidextrous, eventually you will begin to favor one hand, and that will become your dominant hand.

Are you having trouble deciding which hand to use? Ask yourself the following questions:

- Which hand do you consistently use when writing and eating?
- Which hand do you use when tossing or catching a ball?
- Which hand do you use when reaching or using tools?
- Which hand has a natural feel when forming a sign?
- Which hand gives you an extended comfort zone?

As mentioned before, the new signer often feels very awkward and out of control. If you are a natural "righty" or "lefty," do not change your dominant action hand simply because it feels a bit uncomfortable at the start. Give it some time—this feeling is normal and soon dissipates.

Once you have made the decision to be a right-handed or left-handed signer, do your absolute best to be consistent and do not switch back and forth. Constantly changing your dominant hand will only serve to confuse you as you acquire this new skill. This is especially true for new signers.

Some Signs Require Two Hands

Now that you have made your decision to sign with your right hand or left hand, there is a small curve in the road. Not all signs are formed using just one hand. Many signs require the use of both hands, and the use of the dominant hand does not always apply here.

There are three different ways to form signs:

1. **One-handed signs** are formed using only your dominant hand, for example the sign for "mirror."

◀ **MIRROR:** Form the sign for "mirror" by imitating that you are holding a small vanity mirror and looking into it.

2. **Two-handed symmetrical signs** require the use of both hands moving the same and formed with the same handshape. Both hands will also be in the same location. See for example the sign for "rain."

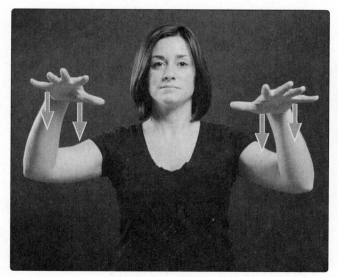

◀ **RAIN:** Form the sign for "rain" with both palms down, fingers spread to an "open five" while dropping your hands down several times to imitate rain.

3. **Two-handed asymmetrical signs** require movement from your dominant active hand while your nondominant hand remains stationary. Often, the nondominant, or motionless, hand acts as a support base in these types of signs. See the signs for "sunrise" and "sunset."

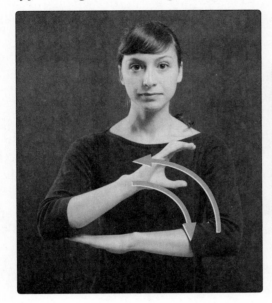

◄ **SUNRISE, SUNSET:** To sign "sunrise," place your nondominant arm and hand level with your chest. With your dominant hand, form the handshape of a, open "C" and bring it upward to a high-noon position; this is "sunrise." Now, bring the arm back down level with the elbow of the nondominant arm, and this represents "sunset."

Look at these images and use the appropriate hand or hands to form the signs just as you see them demonstrated. Now, as a mini-drill, repeat forming these signs three times each. Repetition allows you to gain a feel for the hand and arm movement used in creating these signs. Each one of these three signs should feel quite different from the others as you form each sign. While this may seem a little confusing right now, as you move along and acquire more signed vocabulary, all of what has been discussed here will have greater clarity.

You have signed "mirror" one-handed and "rain" two-handed, using the same movement, direction, and handshape equally. In learning to sign "rain," you have created a two-handed, symmetrical sign. You have signed "sunrise" and "sunset" using your dominant hand to create the action and movement, while your nondominant hand and arm remained motionless. In learning to sign "sunrise" and "sunset," you have created a two-handed, asymmetrical sign. Congratulations—learning these three ways to form signs is a big step!

Strategies

You are fast approaching the chapters that will teach you signed vocabulary for ASL. As you go through the upcoming lessons, you will gain a greater understanding and advance more rapidly if you put the following strategies into place. These strategies also include those that can be applied in the ASL classroom:

- **Practice, practice, practice.** This is the magic key! Form the signs again and again, and set them to memory.
- **Sign slowly with clarity.** Clarity in forming signs far outweighs the importance of the speed. In the study of sign language, the clarity of your signs is your articulation.
- **Don't worry about signing errors.** Errors are all part of the learning process.
- **Don't worry about speed and feeling awkward.** Your speed will improve as you develop control. Learn to form the signs clearly, and add the speed later.
- **Learn to relax while signing.** Simply maintain a relaxed posture, one that is free of bobbing or jerking movements. Remember, this is a visual language, your form is important.
- **Enroll in a sign language course.** A class, this book, *and* interactions with friends and the Deaf community will give you a jump-start into learning conversational ASL.
- **Put aside your English grammar.** How you hear a sentence often is not relative to how a sentence is signed.
- **Learn to see the words versus hearing the words.** ASL is a visual language.
- **Learn to focus on the signer's face, not his hands.**

In order to truly immerse yourself in conversational ASL, beyond this book and the classroom, you need to begin to associate with people in the Deaf community at every opportunity.

Use the signs you know by signing them every day. Try to set aside a short ten minutes a day for review.

Eye Contact

Maintaining eye contact is a firm signing etiquette rule. Breaking eye contact during a signed conversation is considered extremely rude. Learn to develop attentive behaviors during signed conversations, such as nodding and adding an occasional signed exclamation, like "Yes," "Wow," or "Really," just as you would in an oral conversation. In addition, observing the signer's face at all times assists comprehension. Do not worry about focusing on the hands of the signer. Learn to see the whole picture, face and hands simultaneously. Remember, when you don't break that important eye contact, you show interest and respect for the signer. When you are the one who is signing, eye contact is still maintained. Keep in mind that eye contact is a two-way street and a very important element of ASL.

CHAPTER 4

Fingerspelling

Fingerspelling is the letter representation of each of the twenty-six letters of the alphabet. The use of fingerspelling is limited in ASL. It is primarily used to communicate places and names when no formal recognized signs exist. Fingerspelling has very specific rules and only represents about 10 percent of the language's overall elements. However, mastering the manual alphabet is an important complement to ASL. This skill will assist you in understanding the handshapes of the signs you will learn throughout this book. In this chapter, you will find fingerspelling exercises to help you master the manual alphabet.

4

Situations That Call for Fingerspelling

When you don't know a sign for a word, try to describe it by acting it out, pointing, miming, or drawing it. Don't use fingerspelling as your first choice when you don't know a sign. Fingerspelling is not a substitute for signing; it is used for words when a sign does not exist. In ASL, fingerspelling is only used approximately 10 percent of the time and should only be used for:

- Proper names
- Names of towns, cities, and states
- Specific brand names of products or services
- Titles of books and movies

As a word of caution, you should know that new ASL students easily confuse the letters "D" and "F." Use these hints: *flag* for the letter "F" (think of the last three fingers as a mini flag); and *dump* for the letter "D" (*dump* all your fingers on the thumb except for the index finger).

Talking to Yourself

The palm of your hand must always face the receiver/reader when you are fingerspelling. If your palm is facing your chest, then you are talking to yourself, and the receiver cannot read the word or letters you are signing.

In addition, you should never turn your hand away to look at it to make sure you have formed a letter correctly and then turn it back toward the receiver, as this can confuse the receiver. You could describe this situation as having half a conversation with yourself and the other half with the receiver. Simply remember that your palm should always face the receiver.

Becoming an Accurate Fingerspeller

Before forming the letters of the manual alphabet, you'll need to get into the proper position and learn special strategies to become a good fingerspeller.

The following are some tips to ensure accurate fingerspelling:

- Make sure your palm faces the receiver/reader.
- Hold your dominant hand slightly to the right of your face and just below the chin.
- Make sure your elbow is close to your body.
- Do not bounce the letters.
- Relax, and let the letters flow smoothly.
- Speed is not important; it is the clarity of the formation of each letter that matters.
- Do not say or mouth single letters.
- Move slightly to the right or slide slightly to the right for double letters.
- Practice fingerspelling with your elbow resting on a table or desk.

It takes time to get used to fingerspelling and to gain a comfort zone. Try to prevent developing the "bobber-weaver" syndrome and the famous "wing-thing." The "bobber-weaver" syndrome is when the signer fingerspells and moves her wrist and hand position, like a car weaving out of control. This pattern and flow is erratic, making it difficult to comprehend what is being fingerspelled. The "wing-thing" is when the signer, while fingerspelling, constantly lifts her elbow away from the body, as if about to take flight.

To help control and prevent these errors, here are a few tricks that you can learn. During an ASL conversation in which you fingerspell, use your left arm as a support for your right elbow. (If your left hand is dominant, then use your right for support.) This support position is the same as when you formed the signs for "sunrise, sunset" in Chapter 3. Another way to stabilize your hand and arm is to hold your wrist with your left hand, just below the wrist bone. This enables you to immediately feel when your fingerspelling becomes out of control or is starting to take flight. For the novice signer, another less obvious stabilizer is to place the left index finger on the front of the right wrist.

While practicing fingerspelling, try applying these small safeguards for a nice steady and smooth flow. Believe it or not, before you even realize it, you will not need to apply these fingerspelling safeguards at all. In the beginning, though, these serve as control mechanisms that help the novice signer quite nicely.

Hand Warm-Up

When you fingerspell, you will be using your hands in a manner that you're not accustomed to. Therefore, to prevent any discomfort, it's a good idea to do some hand exercises and warm-ups, for example:

1. Shake your hands briskly with your fingers parted.
2. Stretch your hand to an open-finger "five" position until you can feel the skin stretching between each finger.
3. Create a piano strum, starting with your pinky, and ending with your index finger.

Ready? Now, do the previous three exercises one more time. Good! Now you are ready to form the handshapes of the letters of the manual alphabet. Remember, you will be looking at the back of your hand so, try practicing in a mirror.

THE MANUAL ALPHABET (A—C)

▲ **"A" HAND:** Make a fist with your dominant hand, make sure your thumb is on the side of the fist and not within it.

▲ **"B" HAND:** All fingers are vertical and pressed together and your thumb is curled in to your palm.

▲ **"C" HAND:** Form a "C" with all fingers neatly together. Your palm is facing left.

THE MANUAL ALPHABET (D—I)

▲ **"D" HAND:** Curl your fingers down onto your thumb except for the index finger, which remains vertical. *Hint:* "**D**ump" all your fingers on the thumb except the index finger.

▲ **"E" HAND:** Curl all fingers down and tuck the thumb into the palm.

▲ **"F" HAND:** Pinch the index finger to the thumb. Middle, ring, and pinky fingers are vertical. *Hint:* Imagine the last three fingers as a mini flag.

▲ **"G" HAND:** Extend your thumb and index finger facing left, position hand facing slightly left. Middle, ring, and pinky fingers are tucked into palm.

▲ **"H" HAND:** Place your index finger on top of your middle finger facing left, with your thumb tucked away behind the two fingers.

▲ **"I" HAND:** Make a fist, hold your pinky finger vertical.

THE MANUAL ALPHABET (J—O)

▲ **"J" HAND:** Make a fist, hold your pinky finger vertical, and draw a "J" shape inward. *Hint:* "J" is the same handshape as "I" with a simple movement added.

▲ **"K" HAND:** Place your thumb between your index and middle fingers, which are held vertically. Ring and pinky fingers are tucked into the palm.

▲ **"L" HAND:** Make a fist, leave your index finger vertical and extend the thumb.

▲ **"M" HAND:** Tuck your thumb into palm, then wrap your index, middle, and ring fingers over the thumb. *Hint:* Visualize a lowercase "m" with its three lines thus, the three fingers.

▲ **"N" HAND:** Tuck your thumb into palm, then wrap your index and middle fingers over the thumb. *Hint:* Visualize a lowercase "n" with its two lines, thus the two fingers.

▲ **"O" HAND:** Form a nice round "O" by resting all the fingers on the thumb.

THE MANUAL ALPHABET (P—U)

▲ **"P" HAND:** Place your thumb between the index and middle fingers. Ring and pinky fingers are tucked into the palm. Drop your wrist downward. *Hint:* The letter "P" is made the same as the letter "K," except, the P "points" downward.

▲ **"Q" HAND:** Extend your thumb and index finger downward. Tuck middle, ring, and pinky fingers into your palm. *Hint:* The letter "Q" is made like the letter "G," but with the wrist downward.

▲ **"R" HAND:** Cross your index and middle fingers. Thumb, ring, and pinky fingers are tucked into palm.

▲ **"S" HAND:** Make a fist, place your thumb in front of your fingers. *Hint:* The letters "A" and "S" are easily confused. For "A," place your thumb on the side of your fist: for "S," place and "show" your thumb in front of your fingers.

▲ **"T" HAND:** Make a fist. Tuck your thumb between your index and middle fingers.

▲ **"U" HAND:** Hold your index and middle fingers vertical. Tuck your thumb, ring, and pinky fingers into your palm.

THE MANUAL ALPHABET (V—Z)

▲ **"V" HAND:** Your index and middle fingers are held vertical and spread open, creating a "V." Tuck your thumb, ring, and pinky fingers into your palm.

▲ **"W" HAND:** Your index, middle, and ring fingers are held vertical and spread open, creating a "W." Hold your pinky finger down with your thumb.

▲ **"X" HAND:** Make a fist leaving your index finger vertical but bent into a hook shape.

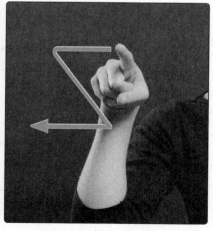

▲ **"Y" HAND:** Extend your thumb and pinky finger. Tuck your index, middle, and ring fingers into your palm.

▲ **"Z" HAND:** Make a fist with your index finger extended, then make the shape of the letter "Z" in the air. *Hint:* Think of "Zorro."

REMEMBER: Did you have the palm of your hand facing you at any time? If you did, then you were talking to yourself. One of the first rules in fingerspelling is: The palm always faces the receiver.

Now, you need to repeat and practice the alphabet two more times. When you feel you have mastered the handshapes of the alphabet, you will be ready to teach it to someone else like a family member, friend, or a coworker. If you teach the alphabet to someone else, you will have a practice partner.

FACT

In 1620, Juan Pablo de Bonnet published the first book that illustrated a manual alphabet, titled *The Simplification of the Letters of the Alphabet*.

Practice Session #1

Get ready! There is still a lot of practice to be done before you are able to master fingerspelling. Using this brief but valuable chart, practice forming the letters by groups:

A, E, O, M, N, S, and T	are formed with a closed hand
B, C, D, F, I, K, L, R, U, V, W, X, and Y	are formed in a vertical position
G and H	are formed in a horizontal position
P and Q	are formed in a downward position
J and Z	are formed with added movement of tracing the letter

The handshapes of the letters of the alphabet vary in degrees from closed to open, and horizontal to vertical. Memorizing the chart will help in your journey to mastering the alphabet. In order to become comfortable and familiar with the handshapes and positions you must practice, practice, practice!

Now for some more practice. "I Love You" is one of the most popular acronym signs and is easily recognized. The characteristics of this handshape are what bring forth the meaning. The vertical pinky represents the letter "I." The index finger and extended thumb represent the "L" in "love." The combination of the pinky and the thumb extended represent the letter "Y" for "you."

◀ **I LOVE YOU:** Combining the letters "I," "L," and "Y" on one hand forms the "I Love You" sign.

When fingerspelling, position your hand in the air slightly to the right of your face. Now, with your hand in this position, imagine standing in front of a refrigerator writing your grocery list on a little magnetized notepad. Use the visual clue of writing on a "notepad" to help you control your fingerspelling.

Practice Session #2

By now, you should be starting to get the feel and look of the handshapes of the letters. Don't forget to do your hand warm-ups before each practice session! Here are some practice ideas to build your fingerspelling skills. Fingerspell the following:

- Names of family
- Street/town names
- Things on the grocery list
- Names you see on trucks, billboards, etc.

The novice signer needs to see and feel these new, manual letters of the alphabet. Hopefully, you have been practicing and are acquiring the feel of each letter. Now that you know how to make the shapes of the letters, move on and find out when to use fingerspelling.

Spelling Bee

It is time to practice fingerspelling three-letter words. The movement from letter to letter will improve the agility of your fingers. Later, you and your fingerspelling partner can practice the spelling bee game together. Haven't found a partner yet? Well, do your best to locate one, and remember: To teach is to relearn.

The instructions for the spelling bee with a partner are as follows. Working from a list, each person alternately and randomly selects a word to fingerspell. The receiver must correctly fingerspell the word back to the sender. Each word is then checked off. Continue in this fashion until you have fingerspelled all the words. Try making the game a little more difficult. Create a new list of fifty words. This time, these words should be four to five letters in length. You can continue playing the spelling bee game in this same fashion by simply increasing the length and difficulty of the words.

cat	mop	top	tap	nap
tip	bag	pit	hat	lip
mug	hit	sip	zip	lug
dim	pie	eye	hug	dye
sag	zap	cap	bit	but
wax	oar	not	get	fit
eat	jar	box	rat	six
van	gin	gym	sir	was
oat	fox	ear	jam	kit
raw	get	jaw	wet	nip

Take It to the Next Level

Next, try this twist on the game. This is similar to deaf/blind interpreting and is a terrific way to really adopt the feel of each letter. You can begin by using words from the same list, like the three-letter word chart presented here as a sample. This time, instead of looking at the letters, each person feels the handshapes of the letters. It begins by having your partner close his eyes while you fingerspell into the palm of your partner's hand. Your partner can use his free hand if he chooses to feel the entire shape of the letters.

This version can be a lot of fun, so give it a try. You will be pleasantly surprised at how quickly you adapt to playing these interesting fingerspelling games. All the games suggested are a great way to practice mastering the alphabet. Don't forget that mastering the alphabet is an important first building block for the novice signer.

Initialized Signs

Initialized signs, also known as borrowed signs, are signs that—in general—borrow the first letter of words. On the facing page is a chart of "initialized" signs. These signed words require placing and/or moving a letter of the manual alphabet in specific locations on or around the body. When you are finished signing this list, you will know twenty-six new initialized signs!

Fingerspelled Loan Signs

Another way the letters of the manual alphabet are used is in the application of fingerspelled "loan signs" and fingerspelled abbreviations. "Loan signs" have unique patterns and movements. They normally have two to five letters, and they are commonly used words. These words are all formed and shaped in various patterns, like so:

- "Bus" is fingerspelled using "B" to "S" in a vertical, downward movement.
- "All" is fingerspelled using "A" to "L" in a sweeping movement from left to right.

Initialized Signs

The Sign	The Letter
Attitude	Tap the "A" hand on the heart.
Boss	Tap the "B" hand on the heart.
Coach	Tap the "C" hand on the top of the right shoulder.
Dentist	Stroke the "D" hand back and forth in front of the teeth.
Elevator	Raise the "E" hand up and down in front of the body.
Feather	Slide the "F" hand over the top of the ear.
Glasses	Stroke the "G" hand along the frame of an imaginary pair of glasses.
Hospital	Use the "H" hand to form a cross on the upper left arm.
Idea	Place the "I" hand on the temple and move forward slightly.
Jeans	Use the "J" hand and trace a "J" movement near the waist/hip area.
King	Tap the "K" hand on the left shoulder, then down on the right hip.
Loser	Place the "L" hand in the middle of the forehead.
Medical	Tap the "M" hand on the inside of the left wrist.
Nurse	Tap the "N" hand on the inside of the left wrist.
Opinion	Place the "O" hand on the temple and move forward slightly.
Prince	Tap the "P" hand on the left shoulder, then down on the right hip.
Queen	Tap the "Q" hand on the left shoulder, then down on the right hip.
Rose	Tap the "R" hand under each nostril.
South	Move the "S" hand straight down.
Toilet	Shake the "T" hand.
Uncle	Hold the "U" hand near the temple and slightly shake back and forth from the wrist.
Vegetable	Tap the "V" hand on each corner of the mouth.
Water	Tap the "W" hand just below the lower lip.
Xylophone	Tap both "X" hands alternately, imitating playing the xylophone.
Yellow	Shake the "Y" hand.
Zoo	Form the letters "Z," "O," and "O," while moving slightly to the right.

- "Dog" is fingerspelled using "D" to "G" as if snapping the fingers.
- "Apt" is fingerspelled using "A," "P," and "T," with a quick down and up flick of the wrist.
- "Refrigerator" is fingerspelled using "R," "E," and "F" in a vertical downward motion.

The loan signs that you have just signed have been developed over a period of time and have proven to be an expedient way of signing these words. These loan signs, through time and by their appearance and movement, have become accepted signs in their loan format. However, for the novice signer, keep in mind these words also have regular whole ASL signs.

Abbreviations and States

Everyday words can quickly be abbreviated applying the manual alphabet. Often, it is manually abbreviated words like these that become the recognized loan signs in time:

- "Air-conditioning" is fingerspelled using "A," and "C" in place.
- "Barbecue" is fingerspelled using "B," "B," and "Q" in place.
- "High School" is fingerspelled using "H," and "S" in place.
- "Identification" is fingerspelled using "I," and "D" in place.
- "Avenue" is fingerspelled using "A," "V," and "E" in place.
- "Boulevard" is fingerspelled using "B," "L," "V," and "D" in place.
- "Overtime" is fingerspelled using "O," and "T" in place.

Of course there are many more abbreviations. Here are three favorites:

- "Videocassette recorder" is fingerspelled using "V," "C," and "R" in place.
- "Compact Disc" is fingerspelled using "C," and "D" in place.
- "Digital Video Disc" is fingerspelled using "D," "V," and "D" in place.

Lastly, here is a cute abbreviation: Form the letter "P." Now trace the letter "Z" in front of you. You've just ordered a "pizza"! This is just one of the many different and fun ways you can sign "pizza."

Abbreviations of States

Mastering the manual alphabet will assist you in the upcoming chapters. The "instructions" on how to form signs often include the various handshapes of letters. Now, here is one more exercise to help you apply your new skill of fingerspelling. Sign each state using its two-letter abbreviation.

State	Abbreviation	State	Abbreviation
Alabama	AL	Montana	MT
Alaska	AK	Nebraska	NE
Arizona	AZ	Nevada	NV
Arkansas	AR	New Hampshire	NH
California	CA	New Jersey	NJ
Colorado	CO	New Mexico	NM
Connecticut	CT	New York	NY
Delaware	DE	North Carolina	NC
Florida	FL	North Dakota	ND
Georgia	GA	Ohio	OH
Hawaii	HI	Oklahoma	OK
Idaho	ID	Oregon	OR
Illinois	IL	Pennsylvania	PA
Indiana	IN	Rhode Island	RI
Iowa	IA	South Carolina	SC
Kansas	KS	South Dakota	SD
Kentucky	KY	Tennessee	TN
Louisiana	LA	Texas	TX
Maine	ME	Utah	UT
Maryland	MD	Vermont	VT
Massachusetts	MA	Virginia	VA
Michigan	MI	Washington	WA
Minnesota	MN	West Virginia	WV
Mississippi	MS	Wisconsin	WI
Missouri	MO	Wyoming	WY

There are various ways to fingerspell the states. Fingerspelling the states, using two letters, is quick and readily recognized. It is also common in ASL to see three or four letters used for state abbreviations. Keep in mind that you will also see regional signs for states. Once you have been shown the regional sign, it is the one that you would use while you are in that region.

ASL has indicators that are often used for acronyms and abbreviations. The signer, while fingerspelling, moves her hand in a small circle. This movement would indicate that what is being fingerspelled should not be read as a regular word. Circular movement can also indicate capitalization.

As you move along in your study of sign language, and as you perhaps become involved with Deaf signers, many points that have been mentioned here will become fine-tuned. Remember, the magic words are *relax*, *enjoy*, and *practice*.

CHAPTER 5

Get a Firm Grip on the Rules

It is important to know the rules governing the proper use of sign language. The explanation of the rules called the "Big Four" will add clarity to the important elements in sign language. Additionally, in this chapter, you will be introduced to intonation, plurals, and a little bit of sign etiquette.

The Big Four

A sign is a unit of language that is formed with distinctive handshapes, locations, specific movements, and facial expressions. The signs have four independent parts. These parts play exacting roles, and if any one of them is changed, the meaning of the sign is altered. Let's take a close look at these four very important parts of signs: Handshape, location, movement, and palm position.

1. Handshape

The term *handshape* refers to the specific shape of your hand while you are forming the sign. The handshapes could be the letters of the alphabet or numbers. Most importantly, most handshapes have specific names; "claw hand," "open five," "flat hand," and so forth. As a novice signer, memorizing the handshape names will be a very important tool: This book, all sign language dictionaries, and ASL instructors use the names of handshapes when giving instruction on how to form a sign.

▲ **ONE HAND:** Hold your index finger upright in the vertical position, palm forward, all other fingers tucked away.

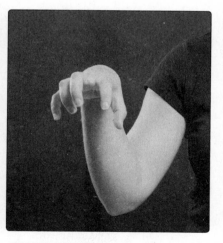

▲ **CLAW HAND:** Bend all your fingers and thumb slightly separated, imitating the shape of a claw.

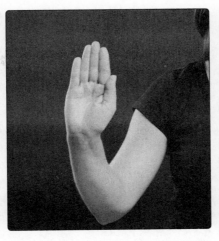

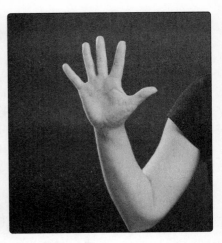

▲ **CURVED HAND:** Make the handshape of "C" and tuck your thumb against the side of your hand.

▲ **FLAT HAND:** Extend all your fingers with your thumb neatly tucked against the side of your hand.

▲ **OPEN FIVE:** Spread apart all your fingers and your thumb.

REMEMBER: Changing the handshape of a sign will change the meaning of a sign, so study these shapes carefully.

▲ **BENT HAND:** Bend your hand at the large knuckles and tuck your thumb against the side of your hand.

▲ **MODIFIED "O/AND" HAND:** Close your hand so all fingers and thumb are touching. Often, this handshape is referred to as the "and" hand.

2. Location

The term *location* describes where you place and form the sign. Location is an important factor because if you change it, you will change the meaning of the sign. The signs for "Mother" and "Father" are a good example of this concept. The sign for "mother" and "father" have the same handshape, an open five. However, the meaning is changed when that same handshape is placed in different locations. The location of these two signs indicates the genders.

▲ **MOTHER:** Tap the thumb of the "open five" hand on the chin.

▲ **FATHER:** Tap the thumb of the "open five" hand on the forehead.

Understanding the importance of location will make your journey into this new language an easy one. The consistency of the principles of ASL also makes your learning curve easier. All female signs will be formed in the jaw line area, though the handshape might be a little different for sister, aunt, or female cousin.

All male signs will be formed in the area of the forehead; although the handshape for brother, uncle, or male cousin may be different, the location does not change.

▲ **MALE:** Move the "modified O" hand slightly away from the forehead. All male signs are made in the area of the forehead. *Hint:* Imitate tipping the brim of a hat.

▲ **FEMALE:** Stoke the extended thumb of the "A" hand down, along the jaw line. All female signs are made in the area of the jaw line. *Hint:* Think of tying a bonnet.

3. Movement

The term *movement* describes the action that makes the sign, such as moving in a circle, up and down, forward or backward. An example would be using the index finger and pointing upward. This movement forms the sign "up." Using the index finger and pointing downward, forms the sign "down." There are many signs just like the ones described, such as in/out and come/go. Simply changing the movement changes the meaning of the sign.

Often, the novice signer incorrectly uses the signs "in" and "out" while signing sentences. Here are a few examples to help you:

- **In:** The correct application for this form of "in," would be if you are putting a pencil "in" a box or, putting contacts "in" your e-mail. The incorrect usage of this sign for "in" would be if it was applied while signing, "in spring." The correct sign would be "during" spring.
- **Out:** The correct application for this form of "out," would be when signing "take the roast "out" of the oven." The incorrect usage of this "out" would be if it was formed while signing, "go out to play."

▲ **IN/OUT:** To sign "in," put the right modified "O" hand into the left "C" hand; to sign "out," pull the right modified "O" hand out of the left "C" hand.

These examples of novice errors are quite common in the early acquisition of ASL. This is one of the reasons why you are encouraged to enroll in an ASL course in addition to learning from this book.

4. Palm Position

The term *palm position* refers to the position of the palms of your hands and the direction the palm is facing. For example, placing your palm on your own chest would mean "my/mine." Facing your palm toward the reader would translate to "your."

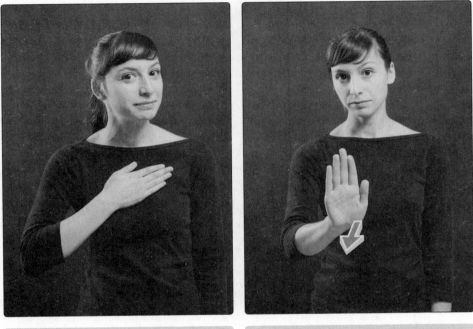

| ▲ **MINE:** Place your "flat" hand, palm inward on your chest. | ▲ **YOUR:** Move your "flat" hand, palm forward, toward the reader. |

You should take a quick look at the following definitions and explanations of the palm positions. You will see these descriptive terms used in this book, ASL dictionaries, and instructional texts.

- "Forward"—Palms are facing away from the body
- "Inward"—Palms are facing toward the body
- "Horizontal"—Palms are parallel to the floor
- "Palm toward palm"—Palms are facing each other
- "Palm-to-palm"—Palms are applied to each other

Recap of the Rules

These Big Four rules of sign are very important elements of sign language. So take a moment to quickly review what you have learned. The first rule is **handshape**. You have learned that the handshape of your hand can change the meaning of a sign. In Chapter 4, you learned about initialized signs. In the practice, there was an instruction to tap the "A" hand on the heart to sign "attitude." However, if you changed the handshape to a "B" hand, the sign changed to "boss." It is a simple concept to remember: Change the handshape, and you change the meaning of the sign. This information is presented to give you a sense of familiarity when you see new and unfamiliar descriptions for signs. Learning any language takes time. The more you are exposed to the terminology, the easier it will be.

FACT

According to the Modern Language Association survey of 2006, college-level enrollment figures in ASL were up dramatically from 11,420 in 1998 to 78,829 in 2006. The most dramatic increase in ASL enrollments occurred between 1998 and 2002, with an increase of 432.2 percent!

The second rule of sign is **location**. Once again, move the location—that is, where you are forming the sign—and the meaning is changed. The third rule is **movement**. Change any movement, and you form a different sign. The fourth rule is the **palm position**. When changed, this too alters the sign's meaning.

Signing Space

The center of the chest is called the sightline. The eyes easily focus on the sightline and at the same time are able to focus on the face, facilitating lip reading and making it easier to observe facial expression.

The signing space, which includes the sightline, is the area where the majority of the signs are formed. This space can be visualized as a pyramid in shape. It starts at the top of the signer's head, goes down past the shoulders, and ends with a horizontal line across the waist. Therefore, when reading signs, look at the person who is signing in this pyramid shape. Keep in mind that the sightline moves with the signer. If while you are signing, you should turn slightly left or right, the sightline will still be the center of your chest.

Reading signs can be tiring, and a signer must consider this. You can lessen eyestrain for the reader by wearing solid-colored clothing. If you have been mulling the possibility of enrolling in an ASL course, keep this in mind. When you are preparing to attend the class, give your wardrobe a second look. It should be solid and free of design. In other words, don't wear shirts with those huge logos in the middle of your sightline.

Intonation

Intonation in sign language is created in a variety of ways. A sign can be formed with intensity to show intonation. For instance, if you worked hard all day, you might form the sign "work" by striking the "S" hands together with noticeable force.

Another way to show intonation is to execute a sign with varying degrees of speed. If you were signing you had to go somewhere in a hurry, you would sign that with a quick snapping motion. On the other hand, if you were just taking a nice slow drive, you would sign that slowly, with the appropriate casual facial expression. Another way of expressing intonation is by using facial expression along with intensity and motion. These elements play an important role in conveying your meaning.

FACT

The longer you sign, the better your skill will become at adding intonation, denotation, and strong visual inflections that enhance your signs. As with all things, these elements just take time and practice to be applied appropriately.

When you want to express that you love something you would sign "love" by gently crossing your arms over your chest. However, if you are madly in love with something or someone, then you would make the same sign tightly, hugging your chest and perhaps rocking back and forth and adding a big delightful smile. These movements, along with your facial expression, instantly add a strong degree to the word "love."

◀ **LOVE:** Cross both arms and hug your chest. This sign can be formed with either closed fists or open palms.

Sign Etiquette

Earlier this chapter discussed the signer's space. A question that is often asked is, "How do I pass through the space between two signers?" The answer is to avoid passing between the signers if at all possible. If it is unavoidable, you simply sign, "excuse," while you quickly walk between the two signers.

Another question that is often asked is, "How do you get the attention of the deaf?" There are several different ways:

- Tap lightly on a shoulder
- Wave a hand
- Flash the lights on and off
- Stomp on the floor
- Rap or tap on the surface of a table

Tapping on a shoulder and waving are the first two preferred ways for getting the attention of the deaf. Please keep in mind that when flashing the lights or stomping on the floor, these would be executed in moderation. If the lights are flashed continuously and rapidly, it could be interpreted as an emergency. The same applies for stomping the feet. In addition, try to avoid nervously strumming on a table if you are with a group of deaf or hard-of-hearing people. This type of behavior could be distracting. Also, chewing gum and long decorated nails only serve as distractions when signing.

◀ **EXCUSE:** Stroke the curved hand, twice, on the left flat palm.

Plurals

There are many different ways to pluralize signs in ASL. Some of the methods are simple, while others require the use of classifiers and numbers. (You will find classifiers described in Chapter 10, and numbers in Chapter 8.) The easiest way to pluralize a sign, for a novice signer, is to simply re-sign it two or more times. For instance, the sign for child, when made multiple times, becomes children.

The following are ways to pluralize signs:

- **Repetition:** Form the sign, repeat the sign to pluralize two, three, or more of the same item.
- **A sweep:** A signer can use the index finger and sweep out and in front of the body to indicate a multiple number, such as "they" or "them," or a flock.
- **Numbers:** Sign the object or thing and add the numbers. (Chapter 8)
- **Quantifiers:** Sign the object and add signs such as "many" or "little."
- **Classifiers:** Sign the object or thing incorporating classifiers, which demonstrate shape, group, quantity, and movement. (Chapter 10)

Sign Order

ASL syntax—that is, sign order—is often difficult to master during the early part of the process of acquiring signing skills. The syntax when signing generally follows this order: object, subject, verb. Time, if applicable, is signed at the beginning of the sentence and often signed again at the end of the sentence. However, ASL syntax is often varied in short sentences. It also varies regionally. For instance, the order could be seen as subject, verb, and object. This is made with modifications, including omitting any "to be" verbs.

FACT

Deaf people rarely leave a room without an explanation, such as getting a drink or going to the bathroom. When a deaf person suddenly leaves a room without an explanation, it is considered rude.

These sign orders may sound peculiar to you. Based on this reason alone, you are encouraged to enroll in a sign language course to socialize with members of the Deaf community. This will help the reasons for the syntactical order of ASL to become clear and fall into place. The transition occurs more quickly when you begin to see language instead of hearing language.

Since this transition takes a while, you can continue to work on sharpening your skills at getting your hands under control, recognizing handshapes, maintaining eye contact, and acquiring sign vocabulary.

Speaking of vocabulary, as you've probably guessed, there is much more in store for you. Learning the rules to any language is difficult. The best advice at this point is do not skip chapters. This book has been written with the novice signer in mind. Each chapter builds upon the next. Take your time, set your own pace, and perhaps reread chapters. Stay focused and this book will give you a strong foundation into the beautiful world of ASL.

CHAPTER 6

Questions, Questions!

Our daily conversations are filled with questions. Therefore, in order to communicate effectively using ASL, you'll need to learn how to ask and receive questions. This chapter will teach you to form questions and apply them with appropriate facial expressions.

Two Types of Questions

The strong visual aspects of sign language require this book to divide questions into two categories. The first category is the "wh-" words: who, what, when, where, why, which, and how. Questions that use these words ask for specific information. The second category is "yes-no" questions. These questions can be answered with a simple yes or no.

Both of these question types need to be supported by specific facial expressions with nonmanual behaviors. Nonmanual behaviors do not use the hands. Instead, these behaviors use the eyes, facial expressions, head movement, body posture, or body language. Signers use nonmanual behaviors to show emotion, emphasize a point, make a negative statement, and ask questions. Facial expressions are equal to vocal intonation. When you do not apply the proper facial expressions and nonmanual behaviors, your questions may not be interpreted correctly.

Applying Nonmanual Behaviors

As a novice signer, your first step toward acquiring the important elements of facial expressions and nonmanual behaviors begins right here, with the two categories of questions. Your first attempts will feel awkward. Be assured that this feeling is quite normal. The skill of applying facial expression and nonmanual behaviors will gradually build and develop naturally as you further your studies in sign language.

Keep in mind that you are in the early chapters of this book. There will be many chances in the following chapters for you to build your skills in sign language.

Wh- Word Questions

When asking a wh- word question, do the following:

- Furrow your eyebrows together
- Tilt your head forward
- Make direct eye contact
- Hold your last sign

Yes-No Questions

When asking a yes-no question, do the following:

- Raise your eyebrows to widen your eyes
- Tilt your head slightly forward
- Make direct eye contact
- Hold the last sign in your sentence

Occasionally, a yes-no question is accompanied by a question mark, as seen in the following example:

▲ **QUESTION MARK:** Use your index finger and trace a question mark exactly as you would write it.

Answering Questions

It's not enough to just be able to ask questions. You'll also need to know how to answer them, or the conversation will be one-sided!

▲ **YES:** Shake the "S" hand up and down. An affirmative head nod should always accompany this sign.

▲ **NO:** Touch your index and middle fingers quickly to your extended thumb. The sign for "no" is small and can be easily missed. A negative headshake should always accompany this sign as it ensures your answer.

Signing Wh- Words

Now it's time to sign the wh- words with the appropriate facial expressions. Get ready, eyebrows down and furrowed, head tilted, and here you go!

ESSENTIAL

Take a minute now and sign the alphabet in order to refresh these handshapes in your mind. Throughout this book, the directions on how to form signs will refer to handshapes, such as the "D" hand or "F" hand. These instructions are simply describing a handshape and generally, there is minimal association with the letter value.

◄ **WHO:** Use the "L" hand and place your thumb in the cleft of your chin and flick the tip of your index finger. *Variation:* Use your index finger and circle your mouth.

◄ **WHAT/HUH?:** Position both right and left "flat" hands, palms up, just above your waist in front of you. Next, move hands horizontally outward and back. Picture this as a double handed karate movement, this is the newest and natural variation of this sign. *Variation (What):* It is important for you to know and recognize the older variation for this sign as it is still used, though becoming infrequent. Extend the index finger of the right hand and draw the fingertip downward across the left "open" palm.

◄ **WHEN:** Hold your left hand with the index finger pointing up, palm facing right. Move your extended right index finger in a clockwise circle around your left index finger. *Variation:* A natural way to sign "when" is to simply shrug the shoulders. Use both right and left hands in "flat" handshapes, palms up, just above the waist in front of you. Next move hands horizontally upward and out in a natural form that would accompany shrugged shoulders.

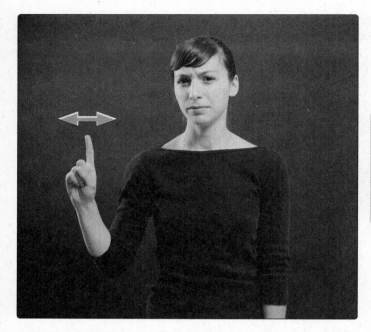

◀ **WHERE:** Repeatedly shake your extended index finger right to left. *Variation:* Use both right and left hands in "flat" handshape, palms up, just above the waist in front of you, hands move back and forth several times displaying frustration.

▲ **WHY:** Place the fingertips on your temple and pull down and out, forming into the letter "Y."

▲ **WHY:** *Variation:* This variation is commonly used; place the fingertips on the temple and pull down and out while wiggling the bent middle finger.

Sign Variations

You will be shown sign variations in the following chapters. Many variations come from regional differences. Sign variations also occur when older signs are reformatted to improve their delivery and make them more expedient. New signs are also developed in order to keep pace with technology.

Early signed communication is depicted in prehistoric cave drawings. These drawings demonstrate that primitive humans were using gestures as a form of communication. In general, just as with all languages, normal changes occur over time. Therefore, be aware that the images shown throughout this book are basic signs. In order to be a good signer, you must be flexible and understand that there can be a variety of ways to form a sign. Presently, "e-mail" is on the top of the list. In this chapter, you will learn two forms for this sign, generic and initialized. In Chapter 15, you will find additional versions for "e-mail."

▲ **E-MAIL:** Pass your right extended index finger through the upheld left "C" hand. This variation is generic.

▲ **E-MAIL:** Form an "E" with your right hand, and form a "C" with your left hand. The "E" hand represents the e-mail. The "C" hand represents the computer. Slide your "E" hand through your "C" hand away from you for outgoing e-mail and toward you for incoming e-mail. This variation is initialized.

The Interview

During your sign language journey, chances are good that you will meet a member of the Deaf community. You will need to be prepared to answer a few questions. It is natural and considered a part of the culture for a member of the Deaf community to ask you several questions. The reason for these many questions is to establish a connection back to the Deaf community.

In early history, when there were people who could not read or write, they were told to sign their name with an X. To this day, we continue to sign our names on the X. The next time you form the sign for "name," lower your hands and look at it from above. Your hands will be in the form of an X.

Next is an interview exercise in which you will sign both the questions and the answers. You will be using signs you just learned from Chapter 5, "my/mine" and "your" in the interview. Now, in order to do this successfully, you need to add a few more signs to your growing vocabulary list.

▲ **INTERVIEW:** Use both "I" hands at each corner of your mouth, and alternately move back and forth from your lips.

▲ **NAME:** Cross and tap the "H" hands twice.

▲ **I, ME:** Use your index finger and point to the center of your chest.

▲ **LIVE/ADDRESS:** Use both "A" hands, palms facing your body, starting at the lower chest and moving upward. *Variation:* Use both "L" hands, palms facing the body, starting at the lower chest and moving upward.

◄ **HOUSE:** Touch the fingertips of the "flat" hands, palms facing and forming a peak, imitating the roof of a house.

◄ **CITY, TOWN, COMMUNITY:** Touch the fingertips of the "flat" hands, palms facing and forming a "peak," tap, and slightly twist several times, imitating multiple roofs. *Variation:* Touch the fingertips of the "flat" hands, palms facing and forming a "peak," tap and separate two or three times while moving the house/buildings to the side.

▲ **WORK:** Use both "S "hands, palms facing down, tap your right wrist on the back of your left fist a few times.

▲ **LEARN:** Place all the fingertips of your right hand into your left palm. Next pull up your right hand with a modified "O" and place it on your forehead. *Note:* The action of the sign suggests putting knowledge into the mind.

▲ **DEAF:** Use your index finger and touch your cheek near the ear, and then near the corner of your mouth.

▲ **MEET:** Hold your right and left index fingers upward, palms facing, then bring the hands together until they meet.

◄ **NICE:** Use right and left "flat" hands, slide the palm of your right hand forward across the left upturned palm, imitating cleaning a counter.

To sign "nice to meet you," combine "nice" and "meet" only. There is no need to sign "you," this information is provided by the directionality of the sign "meet."

The signs for "excuse" and "nice" closely resemble each other and are often confused. "Excuse" is signed with a "curved" hand. "Nice" is signed with a "flat" hand and is also used to sign the word "clean."

E-QUESTION

What is a name sign?
A name sign is used to identify a person and is usually given by a member of the Deaf community. These name signs are often descriptive of that person, and can be visually creative. Once a name sign is given, it eliminates the need of fingerspelling a person's name repeatedly.

Practice an Interview

Looking at the following chart of interview questions, you will notice that the questions are written in English order and then the questions are written in approximate ASL sign order. The answers are presented in a simple ASL sign order. At first, this sign order will sound strange to your auditory ear. You must keep in mind that sign language is a *visual* language. Therefore, how it sounds grammatically is not relative to the way it is received through the eyes. The sign order, as written, is perfectly acceptable. Remember:

- When signing the wh-words, your eyebrows are down and furrowed.
- When answering yes, use a nod.
- When answering no, shake your head.

Adapting to ASL sign order, facial expressions, and nonmanual behaviors are skills that develop slowly with practice and experience. At this point, your primary focus is learning to form the signs accurately, while gradually learning how to apply these additional elements. In order to do this, you will need to practice signing these questions and responses the way they have been written in the chart.

The Interview Questions

English	ASL	Response
What is your name?	Name your?	Name my (fingerspell name)
What city do you live in?	City where live?	Live/address (fingerspell town)
Where do you work?	Work where?	Work (fingerspell workplace)
What is your e-mail address?	E-mail (sign a question mark)	E-mail (fingerspell address)
Where are you learning ASL?	ASL learn where?	ASL learn (fingerspell college)
Are you deaf?	Deaf (sign a question mark)	Yes/No
Nice to meet you.	Nice meet.	Nice-meet-you.

You have just learned how to sign everyday questions and responses! Remember, don't let the ASL order and sound of these sentences concern you. Signing "name my" without the word "is" is perfectly acceptable.

FACT

If you answer that you have a deaf family member or friend, be prepared to provide information regarding the school she attended and the year of her graduation. Deaf people consider school as their home. Since most students lived at schools, fellow students are an extension of their family.

It is important to begin to develop a comfort level. As mentioned earlier, a member of the Deaf community may ask many questions to establish a connection. In doing so, you may be asked these additional questions:

- Do you have a deaf family member?
- Why are you learning sign language?
- Who is your teacher?

Regardless of whether you ever have the experience of meeting a member of the Deaf community, you will still need these everyday question signs.

Rhetorical Questions

The facial expressions and nonmanual behaviors used when asking a rhetorical question include raising the eyebrows and tilting the head to the side and back. However, rhetorical questions are not true questions, and a response is not expected. It is the signer's intention, immediately following this type of question, to supply the answers and information. Rhetorical questions are commonly used in ASL and in the Deaf community. Using this type of question allows a signer to quickly get the attention of others and to introduce a new subject or information.

CHAPTER 7

Variety Is the Spice of Life

Conversation is full of description; it's what adds fun to the otherwise mundane. In this chapter, you will learn how to use descriptions to identify someone and to express your emotions and feelings. In addition, there will be a few dashes of colors thrown in just to make it even more exciting.

Describing People

People are very different from one another. Think of how boring the world would be if everyone were the same! Things like hair color, height, and eye color are all characteristics that distinguish an individual. People use these characteristics to describe others. In sign language, there are certain rules to follow for describing people.

Descriptions of people tend to follow a particular order, and gender is always mentioned first. It is then followed by the height, color of the hair and hairstyle, and body type. If the person being described has any distinguishing features, these can then also be described. For example, someone may have a very large smile, beautiful blue eyes, or perhaps a certain mannerism.

The sign for "face" is formed by circling your face with the index finger. Touching or stroking your hair forms the sign for "hair." When you want to describe someone's hairstyle, you simply mime the hairstyle. Perhaps you have used mime when describing someone with a mustache or beard. Natural gestures serve as wonderful enhancers to signing. It is perfectly okay to use them. In fact, you are encouraged to use natural gestures, facial expressions, and body language.

In the next few sections, you will learn how to sign colors, clothing, and emotions to help you better describe yourself and others.

Color My World

Learning to sign colors in groups according to location (that is, where on the body they are signed) is the best way to put them to memory. All the colors that are signed on the face are described here:

- Pink and red are formed on the lips.
- Brown and tan are stroked on the side of the face.
- Orange is squeezed on the cheek. *Note:* The sign for "orange" can have a different meaning. The hand position near the mouth implies orange juice, while the hand position on the cheek implies the color of orange.
- Black is formed on the eyebrow.

▲ **COLORS:** Wiggle your four fingers slightly at the mouth.

▲ **PINK:** Stroke your middle finger tip of the "P" hand near your lower lip.

▲ **RED:** Stroke your index finger down your lips. *Variation:* Red can also be signed using the letter "R" stroked down the lips. This version is an "initialized" sign.

▲ **BROWN:** Draw the "B" hand down your cheek.

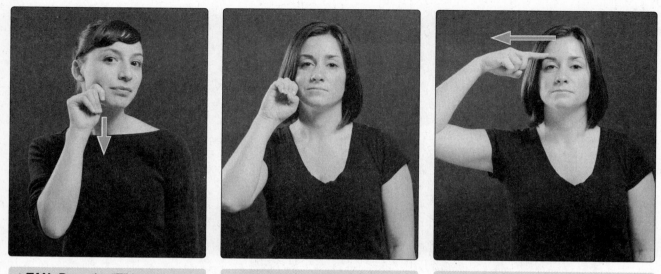

▲ **TAN:** Draw the "T" hand down your cheek.

▲ **ORANGE:** Squeeze the "S" hand in the cheek area.

▲ **BLACK:** Draw your slightly hooked index finger across the eyebrow.

The next set of colors is signed using initializing. These colors are formed in the fingerspelling space with the added element of gently "shaking" the letters.

◄ **BLUE:** Shake the "B" hand gently side to side.

GREEN: Shake the "G" hand gently side to side.

PURPLE: Shake the "P" hand gently side to side

YELLOW: Shake the "Y" hand gently side to side.

◄ **WHITE:** Draw the "open five" hand forward from your chest. Close hand to a modified "O."

The sign for "gray" is a good demonstration of out with the old, and in with the new. The oldest version of "gray" was a combination of three signs. That version was shortened and what was left was a sign best used to describe the concept of gray versus the color. Today's version of "gray" stays in the same sign form as the other colors that are signed in the finger-spelling space, such as yellow and purple. Signing the new way for "gray" is unique. A combination of two letters "G" and "R." are formed on one hand.

◄ **GRAY:** Form the letter "G," then cross your index and middle fingers to form the letter "R," creating a combination of the letters "G" and "R." Shake gently side to side.

Dress Me Up

Your visualization and mime skills will be put to the test in this section as you learn how to describe apparel. First, start with the easy stuff. To sign "shirt," all you need to do is tug on your shirt. See how simple that is! You can describe the sleeve lengths of shirts with visualization. Just extend your left arm and tap at the appropriate length with the side of the "B" hand: Tap the wrist for long sleeves, the forearm for three-quarter-length sleeves, and the upper arm for short sleeves. Generally, you can point to any item of clothing in order to describe it.

Next, visualize a spaghetti-strap top. Now mime sign pulling up the straps. (You know, the kind of top whose straps constantly are sliding off the shoulders.) Still stimulating your visualization and mime skills, let's picture putting on a pair of pants. In order for you to put them on, you need to pull them up. Okay, so guess how you sign pants. If you answered pulling them up to the waist, you are correct! Of course, an outfit wouldn't be complete without a pair of shoes.

ALERT!

Be careful when using one hand for the sign for shirt; one hand means "volunteer." However, if the subject of the conversation is "clothing," then using one hand to sign "shirt" is acceptable.

Today's style of clothing favors the popular T-shirt for comfort and leisure wear. Forming the sign for T-shirt is quick and easy just by using the letter "T" from the alphabet. To sign "T-shirt," stroke the letter "T" downward on the front of your chest.

To sign "shorts," first make the sign for pants then use the edge of both "flat" hands palms up to draw the desired length across the thighs or knees.

▲ **SHOES:** Tap the "S" hands together twice. *Memory aid:* Visualize Dorothy in *The Wizard of Oz* clicking the heels of her shiny ruby red shoes.

▲ **CLOTHES:** Sweep both "open five" hands down over the front of your body once or twice.

◄ **SHIRT, BLOUSE:** Use the index finger and thumb of one or both hands, just below your shoulders, to pinch the fabric and tug forward twice. *Variation:* To sign "blouse," use both index fingers, tap your shoulders, and tap at the waist.

▲ **PANTS:** Place both "open" hands at the waist, and imitate pulling on a pair of pants.

▲ **SKIRT:** Sweep both "open five" hands down from your waist and out to the sides a few times.

▲ **HAT:** Tap the top of your head with a "flat " hand.

▲ **COAT:** Hold the "A" hands in front of your shoulders and imitate putting on a coat with a sweeping downward movement.

They've Got the Look

They say that beauty is in the eye of the beholder. The sign for "beautiful" can be communicated with added emphasis by using your eyes and facial expressions. You have seen, many times on television commercials, in stage performances, and in real life, the natural facial expression that enhances the sign for "beautiful." Try to envision that specific facial expression, the one where the man meets the woman or vice versa, and one or the other is smitten. For instance, you may notice stars in the eyes, rapid blinking, a dazed or dazzled look in the eye, and often a certain tilt to the head.

◀ **LOOK, SEE:** Move the "V" hand forward away from your eye. This sign may be executed with one or both hands and can be moved in the direction of the person or object being "looked" at.

◀ **UGLY:** Use both "X" hands, palms down in front of your mouth and nose, then pull quickly apart. *Variation:* Use only one "X" hand instead of two to lessen the severity.

▲ **BEAUTIFUL:** Use the "open five" hand, starting at your chin, moving clockwise in front of your face, and ending with a closed hand.

▲ **CHUBBY:** Place both "claw" hands on each side of your cheeks.

◄ **THIN:** Use the "G" hand drawn down your cheeks. *Memory aid:* Think of the gaunt cheeks on a slender face.

NOTE: In sign language, using the pinky handshape can represent things that are thin, like lines or spaghetti. This variation is a cute sign and requires good facial expression: Touch both pinky fingertips, palms facing in, and pull apart. Really suck in your cheeks to make them appear gaunt.

The Good and Bad

Now let's look at how you can use sign language to describe your emotions and feelings. As you begin to learn the following signs, it is important to add appropriate facial expressions. When a feeling or emotion is strong, whether it is positive or negative, your facial expression needs to support this information.

▲ **HAPPY:** Place both "flat" hands on your chest and pat with an upward movement several times and smile. Now, add a big or little smile depending on your degree of happiness. This sign, without a smile, makes you a monotone signer.

▲ **SAD, DEPRESSED:** Drop "open five" hands down from your face. In order to have a good facial impact, you need to form the sign while dropping the head and looking sad with sincerity. If you are "depressed," drop the "open five" hands down, with middle finger extended toward your body, from shoulder to waist.

◄ **CRAZY:** Circle the "claw" hand several times at the side of your head. Both hands may be used for this sign to demonstrate intensity. One of the facial expressions that can be used is to somewhat stick your tongue out of the corner of your mouth. *Variation:* To sign "crazy," or "mad about," circle the index finger several times at the temple. Both index fingers may be used for this natural gestural version. The degree of intensity depends on facial expression, such as rolling your eyes around.

▲ **ANGRY, GROUCHY:** Snap the "claw" hand tersely in front of your face. To demonstrate the degree of angry or grouchy scrunch up your face appropriately. *Variation:* To sign "grouchy," "irritable," or "annoyed" move your "claw" hand back and forth in front of your face. Add the appropriate degree of intensity on your face. To accomplish this, you can raise an eyebrow, if you have long hair, flip your hair back, or make a big sigh.

▲ **PROUD:** Draw the "A" hand straight up your chest. Add the appropriate body language: straight back, head up, chin out.

▲ **LONELY:** Draw the index finger of the "one" hand down your chin. Add the appropriate facial expression by looking downward with a slightly sad face.

▲ **SMILE:** Use both index fingers of the "one" hands and draw a smile up and away from your mouth. Flash a big smile while forming this sign! *Variation:* To demonstrate a large smile draw both "B" hands up and away from the mouth, imitating a "smiley face."

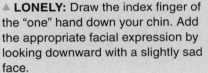

▲ **TIRED:** To sign "tired," drop "bent" hands slightly at center of your chest and lean forward with a look of droopy eyes.

▲ **FUNNY:** To sign "funny," brush the index and middle fingers off the side of your nose. This sign needs a little smile to be believable.

Pronouns and Possessives

If you have the opportunity to go to a social event in the Deaf community, you will see a room come alive with signs, natural gestures, facial expressions, and body language. The Deaf are fabulous storytellers and easily capture your attention with the full animation that rounds out their storytelling. Depending on your interest and the application of your ASL skills, someday you may find yourself signing a story. Chapter 6 has just shown you the basic signs for asking questions and making introductions. Let's learn possessives and a few pronouns to continue building your ASL skills.

▲ **YOU:** Point the index finger of the "one" hand toward the person. In sign language, pointing is referred to as "indexing." This is an appropriate and important element in this visual language.

To sign "they" "them" "these" "those," use the same sign form as "you," adding a sweeping movement in the direction of the objects or subjects.

▲ **US, WE:** Use the handshape of "K," palm facing your right shoulder, extend your arm back and forth. The sign for "we" and "us" uses a form of indexing. Instead of pointing to the person and then to yourself, this sign simply swings back and forth between you and an imaginary or real person. *Variation:* To sign "we," tap the index finger of the "one" hand on the right shoulder then sweep across the chest and tap the left shoulder.

Possessives

In Chapter 5, you learned how to form two possessive signs "my/mine" and "your." This chapter will extend the application and uses for the sign "your." If you have forgotten how to form this sign, return to the chapter and take a quick look at the image. To begin, sign "your," which is the basic root sign for yours, theirs, his, and hers. To sign all of these words, all you need to do is make a few directional changes and/or add a sign.

- To sign "your," use the "flat" hand, palm facing forward, extend the arm forward toward the person. This sign is the root for the following signs.
- To sign "yours," "theirs," use the "flat" hand for "your," palm facing forward, now move your hand with an extended arm left to right across the front of your body.

Should you have a need to be gender specific, you are now ready to learn how to sign "his" and "hers." The signs for "his" and "hers" are compound signs. A compound sign uses two or more signs to convey an idea.

- To indicate "his," sign "male" first, followed by the sign for "your."
- To indicate "hers," sign "female" first, followed by the sign for "your."

◄ **THING, THINGS:** Move the "flat" hand, palm up, forward and slightly to the right.

If you have lots of things, what-cha-ma-call-its, or thing-a-ma-bobs, simply swing out your right hand and then your left hand. You can also add small up-and-down bobble movements when moving this sign, demonstrating "lots of stuff."

The possessive signs you have just learned are important and used frequently in our daily conversations.

You have come to the end of this chapter, and you have come a long way. In this chapter alone, you have learned over thirty-five new signs! Try signing them once again to etch them better into your memory.

CHAPTER 8

Count 1-2-3

This chapter will introduce simple numbers and give you a guideline to master the basic formations. You will learn to form signed numbers with ease and quickly be counting up to a million on one hand. Along the way, you'll also learn how to sign fractions and signs related to money.

8

It's All in the Numbers

You use many different kinds of numbers in your daily conversation. For instance, a conversation might include a phone number, credit card number, and so forth. Now it's time for you to learn how to use numbers in ASL.

Unfortunately, a novice signer often feels that numbers are confusing and somewhat complicated. In order to minimize confusion, this chapter will take a look at examples of numbers that seem to be the pitfalls for new signers. These particular numbers are the ones that share the same hand-shapes as the letters of the alphabet, thus causing the confusion. The context of a conversation generally adds the clarity that is needed to distinguish between a signed number and letter.

Counting to Ten

Counting to ten is easy. You have been doing this since you were a child. In this case, however, there is one difference. When you were a child, you had to use two hands to count this high. In sign language, you can count to ten (and much higher) using just one hand! A starting place for the material covered in this chapter is to learn to sign "number," and the sign for "0" (zero).

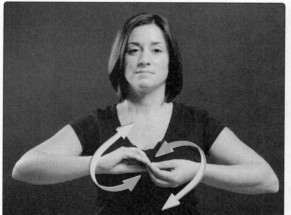

▲ **NUMBER:** Touch the fingertips of both flattened "O" hands, and pivot back and forth alternately.

▲ **ZERO:** Form the letter "O," palm facing left. The sign for the number "0" will be used in forming other numbers.

One Through Five

With a quick look at the images, you should be able to duplicate the individual handshape of numbers "1" through "5." The number "3" requires the vertical extension of your thumb along with your index and middle fingers. The handshape for the number "5" is referred to as the "open five."

▲ **ONE:** Hold your index finger upright in the vertical position, palm forward, all other fingers tucked away.

▲ **TWO:** Hold your index and middle fingers slightly spread apart, upright in the vertical position, palm forward, all other fingers tucked away.

▲ **THREE:** Hold your index finger, middle finger, and thumb slightly spread apart, upright in the vertical position, palm forward, all other fingers tucked away.

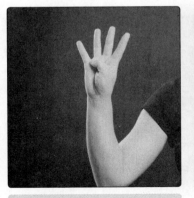

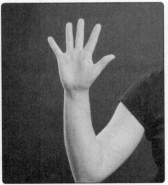

▲ **FOUR:** Hold your index, middle, ring, and pinky fingers apart, in the vertical position, palm forward, and thumb tucked into the palm.

▲ **FIVE:** Hold all fingers spread apart, upright in the vertical position, palm forward.

NOTE: Your flexibility as a new signer really counts in this chapter. Tips and visual examples are right here to support you.

Six Through Ten

The counting process changes for six through nine. It's easy; you only need to touch a specific finger to your thumb.

▲ **SIX:** Touch your pinky finger to your thumb. *Note:* The number "6" looks like a "W." The context of a conversation will help you to differentiate between numbers and letters.

▲ **SEVEN:** Touch your ring finger to your thumb.

▲ **EIGHT:** Touch your middle finger to your thumb.

▲ **NINE:** Touch your index finger to your thumb. *Note:* If you're thinking that the number "9" is another example of duplicity, you're right again. It has the same handshape as the letter "F."

▲ **TEN:** Extend your thumb on the "A" hand and pivot your wrist to the right.

REMEMBER: When signing the numbers six through nine, hold the remaining fingers upright, and have your palm facing forward. Just think, there is no need to use both hands to count above five again!

Time to Review

You made it to ten counting on one hand! Let's do a quick review of how you accomplished this. In sign language, the pinky finger represents the number "6." The ring finger represents the number "7." The middle finger represents the number "8." The index finger represents the number "9." When you lightly touch any of these four fingers separately to the thumb, this action confirms the number position. Simply refer to the table at the right until you master the numbers. Here is another memory aid to help you: Little finger, little number; big finger, big number.

Number	Finger Position
6	pinky
7	ring
8	middle
9	index
10	thumb

Now, let's examine those numbers and letters that share the same hand-shapes and that are the cause of some confusion for novice signers:

- The number "2" is formed in the same way as the letter "V."
- The number "6" is formed in the same way as the letter "W."
- The number "9" is formed in the same way as the letter "F."
- The number "10" is formed in the same way as the letter "A," but with the addition of a twist of the wrist.

FACT

The way numbers are signed can vary according to region. In some regions, the numbers are signed with the palms facing you; in others, the palm is facing the reader. Both palm positions are correct, depending on your geographical region and perhaps on your ASL teacher as well.

Number Handshapes as Descriptors

You will find that the handshapes of numbers are also used as descriptors. Instructions in sign language dictionaries often refer to numbers to describe handshapes. For example, you may see entries that tell you to use the "one" hand or to use the "three" hand. In previous pages of this book, you have already read instructions on forming a sign that used the handshape of a number: an "open five" hand. Knowing how to form all the handshapes, including numbers, is a very important part of your new journey into this visual language.

Conversations with Letters and Numbers

When a conversation occurs that requires both letters and numbers, such as a password or an e-mail address, the dilemma can be resolved in two easy ways. The first solution is to slightly shake the numbers back and forth while maintaining a smooth flow for the letters. This slight movement helps to establish that you are signing a number and not a letter. The second solution is to sign all numbers with the palm facing you and all letters with the palm facing the reader. Of these two methods, the first one, shaking the numbers, is the easiest for the novice signer.

ESSENTIAL

As mentioned earlier, numbers in sign language have many different variations. Simply master the basic numbers, and you will successfully get through any conversations requiring signed numbers. Remember, learn the basics and stay flexible; numbers can change from region to region, signer to signer.

Tackling Eleven Through Nineteen

Now it's time to move on and learn the next section of numbers. As a memory guide to help you along, the numbers "11" through "15" will be referred to as the "flicks." (You'll see why in just a moment.) Look back at the images of "1" through "5" and set them in your mind. The reason; numbers "11" to "15" use the same handshapes as numbers "1" through "5."

Now, one at time, form the same handshapes for each number and simply "flick" the appropriate fingers *twice*. These numbers are formed with the *palm facing you*. The index finger is flicked for eleven. The index and middle finger are flicked for twelve. Continue to do the same right through fifteen. It's easy!

◄ **ELEVEN:** With your palm facing you, flick your index finger twice.

- To sign "12," palm facing you, flick your index and middle fingers twice.
- To sign "13," palm facing you, flick your thumb, index, and middle fingers twice.
- To sign "14," palm facing you, flick your index, middle, ring, and pinky fingers twice.
- To sign "15," palm facing you, flick the "open five" hand.

ALERT!

There is a variation in signing "16" through "19." Some people form these number signs by starting with signing the number "10" then adding a "6," "7," "8," or "9."

Moving right along, let's take on numbers "16" through "19," which are referred to as the "swing-outs." The good news is that the finger positions for numbers that contain a "6" through "9" remain constant. These numbers begin with the palm facing you and then swing out to the right ending with the palm facing forward. Forming the number "16" begins by touching the thumb to the pinky, palm facing you, then swinging out to face the receiver. The numbers "17" through "19" are formed in the same manner, by first touching your thumb to the appropriate fingers then swinging out.

◄ SIXTEEN: Touch your thumb to your pinky, palm facing you, then swing your hand out to the right, ending with palm forward.

- To sign "17," touch your thumb to your ring finger, palm facing you, then swing your hand out to the right, ending with palm forward.
- To sign "18," touch your thumb to your middle finger, palm facing you, then swing your hand out to the right, ending with palm forward.
- To sign "19," touch your thumb to your index finger, palm facing you, then swing your hand out to the right, ending with palm forward.

ESSENTIAL

Keep in mind that these instructions have been simplified in order to give you a survival guide to signing numbers. When you journey further into your studies of sign language, you will be exposed to a multitude of variations when it comes to signing numbers. Nonetheless, by mastering the basics shown in this chapter, you will have a wonderful head start.

Counting to Ninety

You made it through two whole sets of numbers! To reward you for all your hard work, you'll now finish off with easier numbers. If you take your sign language studies further, such as enrolling in a sign language course, you will learn that there are a few shortcuts to numbers. However, for now, all you need is to master the basic numbers.

◀ **TWENTY:** Use your index and thumb only, all other fingers tucked away. Bring your index finger and thumb together while slightly pulling back.

The sign for "20" is a stand-alone sign. In order to form the handshapes for the numbers "30,""40,""50," "60," "70,""80," and "90," you will need to sign the basic number first, such as "3," "4," or "5." You will then sign a "0" (zero). A memory aid for these numbers is an easy formula: The number then changes to zero. Take a look at the following example.

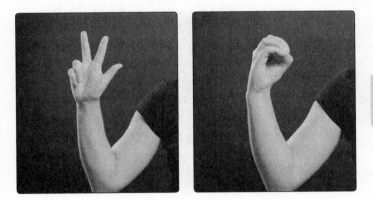

◀ **THIRTY:** Sign the number "3," then a zero, "0."

- To sign "40," sign the number "4," then "0."
- To sign "50," sign the number "5," then "0."
- To sign "60," sign the number "6," then "0."
- To sign "70," sign the number "7," then "0."
- To sign "80," sign the number "8," then "0."
- To sign "90," sign the number "9," then "0."

Big Numbers

You have made it all the way up to "99." Now you will begin working on large numbers. The big numbers—hundreds, thousands, millions—require the simple application of modified Roman numerals. These signs are compound signs. The letter "C" represents the Roman numeral for "hundred." When you want to sign a number in the hundreds, you form the number, then add the letter "C." For example, if you sign "1" then the letter "C" this equals "100." You can continue in the same pattern for "200," "300," "400," and so on. A good memory aid: A hundred-dollar bill is often referred to as a "C note."

▲ **HUNDRED:** Place the letter "C" in the left palm.

The letter "M" represents the Roman numeral for "thousand." When you want to sign a number in the thousands you form the number, and add the letter "M." It is the same pattern that you use for forming numbers in the hundreds. A "million" is signed by tapping the letter "M" twice in the palm.

▲ **THOUSAND:** Tap the extended fingers of the letter "M" once in your left palm.

Fractions

Fractions are signed exactly the way they appear, one number over the other. First sign the top number, the numerator, followed by the bottom number, the denominator. In this example, the visual of a "1" above a "2" demonstrates a numeric fraction. Use this same pattern and order of signs for all fractions.

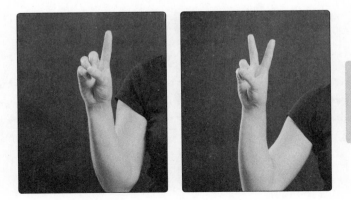

◀ **ONE-HALF:** Form the handshape "1," move hand down slightly and change to the handshape of "2."

Money

Now it's time to combine your basic numbers with money-related signs. Everyone likes to have money, and the first sign indicates that money is in your hand.

▲ **MONEY:** To sign "money," tap the back of the modified "O" hand on your left palm several times.

▲ **RICH:** First sign "money," then change the handshape to a down-turned "claw" hand, and pull up, representing a stack of money. *Note:* The higher you raise the stack, the richer you are. This is another example of a compound sign.

E-QUESTION

What is the sign for "bank"?
Surprisingly, the word "bank" is often fingerspelled. The use of ATM cards for banking purposes has sparked a change for this sign. Today, if you are using your ATM card, you can fingerspell "ATM" and/or mime putting your ATM card into the teller machine.

◀ **BANK:** Slide the right "B" hand, palm up, between the thumb and palm of the down-turned left "B" hand. *Hint:* Visualize sliding a deposit envelope into an ATM machine.

▲ **POOR:** Place the "open five" hand on your elbow and pull down to a modified "O." Visualize holes in your elbow sleeve.

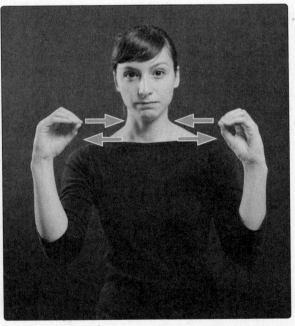

▲ **NONE:** Use both hands, form the sign for "0" (zero), move hands apart. This movement can be made several time to show degree.

▲ **TAX, COST, PRICE:** Draw the "X" hand down your left palm.

▲ **PROFIT:** Move the "F" hand down over your heart, imitating placing money in a pocket.

◀ **SELL, SALE:** Use the modified "O," bend both wrists downward and pivot forward once.

"SHOP" or "STORE": Use the modified "O," bend both wrists downward and pivot back and forth with a double motion. A cute memory aid for "shopping" is to imagine carrying bags, and they are swinging back and forth.

◀ **DOLLAR:** Grasp the fingers of your palm-up left hand with your right hand and pull away.

▲ **OWE:** Tap the tip of your index finger into your left palm several times.

▲ **PAY:** Place your index finger on your left palm, snap the index finger off the palm pointing forward or directionally. *Variation:* Slide the "P" hand off the left palm.

Signing Everyday Numbers

Numbers fill your daily life. To help manage all those numbers, an easy rule to follow is to sign numbers exactly the way they are spoken. When you want to tell someone your phone number, you will sign numbers in groups as they are written. Phone numbers are grouped with the area code first, followed by three numbers, then by four numbers. To sign your phone number, simply hesitate just a bit in between each group of numbers: "555" (hesitate), "555" (hesitate), "5555." Don't drop your hands; just hesitate.

Often, when discussing money in an ASL conversation, you will see "dollar" signed first, followed by the amount. This may sound strange, but look at how you actually write dollar amounts: $19.00. You always write the dollar sign first, so it's not so strange after all!

Here is an example of the three different ways you could sign the number "1,900."

1. When referring to "1900" as "nineteen hundred," sign "19," followed by the letter "C," representing the Roman numeral for 100.
2. When signing "1900" to represent "one thousand nine hundred," sign "1," followed by "M," representing the Roman numeral for 1,000, then "9," followed by "C." Memory aid: Numbers are signed the way you say them.
3. When signing "1900" to represent "nineteen dollars" (or $19.00), sign "19" then "dollars." You can also sign "money" or "dollar" first, then "19."

CHAPTER 9

Friends, Family, and Acquaintances

Now that you know some signs to help you describe people, you're going to take that knowledge a step further and add genders and relationships. Once you are finished with this chapter, you will be able to identify specific members of your family, such as an aunt or brother, and also have the tools to be able to begin signing some occupations.

Genders

The sign vocabulary that you are acquiring is becoming larger with each chapter. In previous chapters, you may have noticed that some of the signs were repeated, but the repetition featured a slight variation that changed the meaning of the sign. Most of the changes in these images are subtle and are described in the text or shown with arrows. Some of the signs were the same, but they had two different meanings depending on the context of the sentence. This book shows you repetition in order to include the sign in new groups of signs with new meanings. In some instances, this is to show you that one of the best tools a signer can have is a large batch of synonyms. They are wonderful tools!

As an example, the sign for "male" can also be "sir," "man," "gentleman," "guy," or "boy." The sign for "female" can also mean "miss," "madam," "ma'am," "woman," "lady," or "girl." You could be in a place of business and say, "Excuse me, Sir," or "Excuse me, Miss" to the clerk. These expressions would still be signed using the same signs for "male" or "female," as shown in Chapter 5.

Gender is easy to specify: All female signs are formed by stroking the jaw line. All male signs are signed from the forehead. Here are two excellent memory aids:

- **Male:** Visualize tipping the brim of a baseball hat.
- **Female:** Visualize tying the strings of a bonnet.

The next set of signs involves gender. Before beginning, it is worth revisiting Chapter 5 to look again at the images for "male" and "female."

Family Relationships

Next, you'll learn how to be more specific with gender signs. In general, you will learn to sign gender first followed by a second sign that is appropriate to the meaning or the clarification. Once again, a series of two or more signs is called a compound sign. Let's begin with the sign for "family," which demonstrates unity.

◄ **FAMILY:** Hold the "F" hands close to your body, thumb tips touching, move both hands out in a circular movement until both sides of your pinky fingers touch.

Now that you know how to sign "family," using the same form you can also sign "team" using the letter "T," "class" using the letter "C," and "group" using the letter "G."

◄ **CHILD:** The sign for "child" can indicate various ages. Just extend your arm, and raise it to the age-appropriate height.

If you want to sign "children," all you need to do is pat the heads of several imaginary "children" all around you.

Signing "baby" or "infant" is easy. It is a natural gesture. You need only to imitate holding and rocking a baby in your arms.

The signs for Father and Mother were introduced in Chapter 5. Now, here are common variations to these two signs:

- **Variation on father:** To sign "father," place the thumb of your "open five" hand on your forehead and wiggle your fingers.
- **Variation on mother:** Place the thumb of your "open five" hand on your jawline and wiggle your fingers.

To sign "parents," first sign "mother" and then immediately sign "father." These two signs create the compound sign for "parents." A variation is to tap the "P" hand above and below your cheekbone. Using the "P" hand to sign "parents" is an example of an initialized sign. In fact, if you use the "A" hand in place of the "P" hand, you are now signing the word for "adults."

Signing "grandfather" and "grandmother" is easy. You will only need to add a forward movement.

- **To sign grandfather:** First sign "father," then move forward with a large arched movement off your forehead. This movement indicates generations. *Variation:* First sign "father," then move forward with two small arcs off your forehead.
- **To sign grandmother:** First sign "mother," then move forward with a large arched movement off your forehead. *Variation:* First sign "mother," then move forward with two small arcs off your forehead.

◄ **MARRIAGE:** To sign "marriage," tightly seal both hands together, representing a bond.

Now that you have learned how to sign "marriage," you are able to form the compound sign for "husband" and "wife." To form these signs, you will need to sign the gender first, then the sign for "marriage." In other words, sign "female" and "marriage" for "wife." Sign "male" and "marriage" for "husband."

The signs for "brother" and "sister" are also compound signs. This image demonstrates the faster and more popular variation.

▲ **BROTHER:** Tap the slightly extended thumb tip of the right "G" hand on your forehead, bring your right hand down, and place it on the left "G" hand in front of your body.

▲ **SISTER:** Tap the slightly extended thumb tip of the right "G" hand on your jawline, bring your right hand down, and place it on the left "G" hand in front of your body.

By now, you should have mastered the location of the female and male signs. Having mastered genders, you can easily sign the remaining family members. These signs are initialized in their appropriate gender locations:

- **Uncle:** Hold the "U" hand near your temple and shake slightly back and forth from your wrist.
- **Nephew:** Extend the fingers of the "N" hand toward your temple and shake slightly back and forth from your wrist.
- **Niece:** Extend the fingers of the "N" hand toward your jaw line and shake slightly back and forth from your wrist.
- **Aunt:** Hold the "A" hand near your jaw line and shake slightly back and forth from your wrist.

People You Know

You will now learn to affix the "person" sign to create compound signs used to describe people. (Of course, the "person" sign can also be used alone to simply mean "person.") Learning to affix or apply the "person" sign gives you a powerful tool for communication. When the "person" sign is used as an ending, it can be referred to in sign language dictionaries as any of the following: "person," "agent," or the "er" sign. We will refer to it as the "person" sign.

When the "person" sign is applied to a sign, it is now considered a compound sign and adds clarity. This compound sign identifies whether you are talking about an item or a person. For example, you can imitate playing the piano, and this is clearly understood when signed. However, if you want to sign "pianist," you imitate playing a "piano" then add the "person" sign. Another example is to sign "write" then add the "person" sign to signify that you mean "writer" or "author." In Chapter 11, where you will learn to sign about sports, you will have many opportunities to apply the "person" sign. With one sign, you can change a sport into the "player" of that sport.

Two for One

In this section, you will learn to sign vocabulary words simultaneously. First, you will learn to sign a noun or verb. Next, you will sign that noun or verb followed by the "person" sign. The signs for interpreter, teacher, and lawyer (on the facing page) require adding the "person" sign.

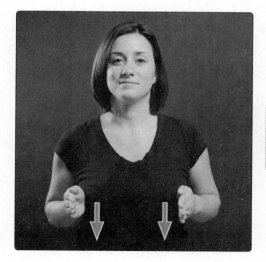

◀ **PERSON:** Use both "flat" hands, palms facing each other, and move hands straight down in front of your body.

◀ **INTERPRET:** Twist the "F" hands alternately back and forth. To sign "interpreter," twist the "F" hands alternately back and forth, and add the "person" sign. *Memory aid:* The movement of the hands depicts translating back and forth between people.

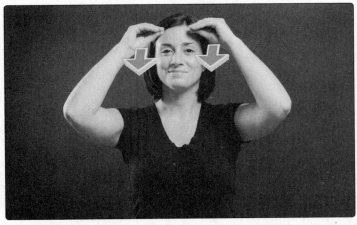

◀ **TEACH:** Move both modified "O" hands forward from your forehead. To sign "teacher," move both modified "O" hands forward from your forehead, and add the "person" sign. *Memory aid:* The hands moving forward from your forehead represents taking knowledge from the mind and giving it forth to the learners.

◀ **LAW:** Slide the right "L" hand in the left vertical hand from the fingertips to your wrist. To sign "lawyer," slide the right "L" hand in the left vertical hand from the fingertips to your wrist, and add the "person" sign. *Memory aid:* The "L" in the hand represents the book of Laws and Rules.

Not all signs affix or use the "person" sign to refer to occupations or sports. Here you will also learn a few signs that do not require affixing the "person" sign. For example, the signs for "dentist" are representative of how nicely signs evolve with the change in times. Hitting your jaw line with the "S" hand was an early sign. This sign represented silver being hammered into teeth for fillings or a very bad toothache. This version is used for a bad toothache. Next, the generic version is tapping a tooth with the index finger then adding the "person" sign. Another version is the initialized sign, which has you tap your teeth with the "D" hand. Today, there is a brighter smiling variation of "dentist." This sign reflects the new attitude of painless dentistry and the bright white smile of healthy teeth.

Dentists, as with other medical personnel, should use "clear" masks when servicing deaf or hard-of-hearing patients. The clear mask allows patients to lip-read. This small change to clear masks by dentists and their staff improves communication and reduces unintentional barriers.

▲ **DENTIST:** Smile while moving the "D" hand slightly back and forth in forth in front of your teeth.

▲ **FIRE FIGHTER:** Place the "flat" hand, palm forward on your forehead. *Memory aid:* The hand-shape represents the shield emblem on the helmet.

The Workplace and the ADA

The Americans with Disabilities Act, or ADA, has the potential to affect workplaces. Today, many businesses eagerly hire applicants who have sign language on their resumes, especially in the arenas of education, medical, and law enforcement. "Public accommodations" is a broad term, as mandated by the ADA, and there is a good chance it may be enforced where you are currently employed. Here are a few examples of workplaces the ADA affects:

- Shopping malls, stadiums, museums, and libraries
- Hospitals, health centers, courts and social services
- Public transportation, and airlines
- Public and private education, and law enforcement agencies

◄ **POLICE OFFICER:** To sign "police officer," tap the "C" hand over the heart, representing the officer's badge.

If you are interested in the political sciences, law enforcement, state, local, or federal, it would benefit you to have the skill of ASL. The need for law enforcement agencies and first responders to have knowledge of basic sign language grows each year.

FACT

The ADA affects nearly everything law enforcement agencies do, such as arresting, booking, and holding suspects. As an example, when a deaf person whose predominant language is ASL is arrested, the ADA ensures that they receive a careful explanation of the Miranda Rights by a qualified sign language interpreter and have reasonable accommodations allowing them to communicate.

To round out the chapter, this last sign is an important acquisition to your sign vocabulary no matter your workplace. The sign is "disability." To sign "disability," begin with the letter "D," changing to the letter "A" while moving in a small clockwise circle.

CHAPTER 10

The Whole Picture

Facial expressions are an important element of ASL. This chapter introduces this element with images for you to view and learn. Body language will be discussed, and classifiers will be introduced as well. All of these elements serve to build your skills toward becoming a well-rounded and knowledgeable signer.

A Face Is Worth a Thousand Signs

Facial expressions make a world of difference, not only in sign language but also in everyday conversations. A simple frown or a tilt of the head can change or enhance conversations. In sign language, facial expressions are a part of nonmanual behaviors. In other words, they are not signs.

You can compare nonmanual behaviors to a person's mannerisms. These types of mannerisms simply happen and one doesn't think about them to produce them. The novice signer often has difficulty applying facial expressions and nonmanual behaviors because at first they seem extreme. However, if you were to videotape a natural conversation, you would see that facial expressions occur throughout a conversation.

For example, consider the case of a friend telling you that another friend had been in a car accident. Your reply might be, "What! Is he okay?" Your natural expression for "What!" would likely be a look of shock. Your eyes would widen, and your head might tip forward or back. The second part, "Is he okay?" might be accompanied by an expression of concern. These types of everyday facial expressions occur naturally. You apply them constantly without even thinking.

ALERT!

In sign language, if you do not communicate with facial expressions, you are considered a boring signer. Lack of facial expression is the ASL equivalent of speaking in a monotone voice.

In Chapter 6, you were introduced to facial expressions that accompany the "wh-" words. In Chapter 7, you learned how to sign words that express emotion and, at the same time, how to apply the appropriate degree of facial expression. Now it's time to try a few more. View the following images, and note the facial expressions of the model. Then try it. Remember, you already know how to smile, frown, or look grouchy. The goal with these images is to sign each one with the appropriate facial expression.

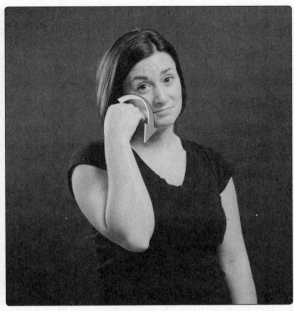

▲ **SORRY:** Rotate the "A" hand clockwise in the middle of your chest. A slight tilt of your head, a small, sheepish smile, or a little pouty smile are good facial expressions for this sign.

▲ **SHY:** Brush the back of the fingers of the "bent" hand against the cheek in a forward arc movement. Enhance this sign by having a bowed head and eyes downward.

◀ **CRY, TEAR:** Draw the index fingers down your cheeks beneath your eyes several times. To demonstrate one tear, use only one finger. *Variations:* Draw both "four" handshapes down your cheeks beneath the eyes several times. This shows an abundance of tears, adding emotional depth to the sign. This version would be the equivalent of "sobbing." Add a pouting or sorrowful facial expression to enhance this sign.

◀ **FEAR, AFRAID:** Holding both "S" hands on the sides of your body, thrust the hands to an "open five" in front of your body. The sign for fear is enhanced by the degree of intensity on your face. Your eyes should be widened and your mouth open.

▲ **JEALOUS, ENVY:** Twist your pinky forward near the corner of your mouth. Add a facial expression of squinting eyes and pursed lips. *Variation:* To sign "envy," twist the index finger forward near the corner of the mouth.

▲ **EMBARRASSED:** Move "open five" hands up and down alternately in front of your face. Tilt your head and add a sheepish smile. *Variation:* To sign "blush" move both "bent" hands up the sides of your face. Both versions can be used with shrugged shoulders and a head tilt.

Lean into It with Body Language

Everyone likes a story, and people love to tell their own. Children adore listening to and watching stories. If you want to become a good storyteller, use appropriate animated facial expressions, body language, and mime. In addition, you can use role-playing methods.

Role-Playing Using Facial and Body Language

Imagine you're telling a story that has two characters, one on your left and one on your right. Simply apply a body shift to represent the position of these characters. To body shift, just turn your torso. Let us imagine that your story characters are an ogre and a princess. In order to demonstrate these characters, put the ogre on the right and the princess on the left. When you turn your torso to the right, adopt the ogre's character with a big, upright chest puffed out. When you turn left, adopt a soft, sweet feminine posture.

Throughout your story use an appropriate eye gaze that models the characters' perspectives. For instance, when the ogre speaks to the princess, look left with the appropriate eye gaze for his character. Without even realizing it, your facial and body language can convey a concept: the ogre's infatuation with the lovely princess. The secret is in the eyes—blink repeatedly, fluttering your eyelashes while slightly swaying back and forth.

Storytelling with Style

If you are a professional who works with young children, have children of your own, or have friends who like to have fun, try imitating two characters in the manner described. Your audience will be delighted with this type of visual enhancement. When you first begin to practice role-playing, you don't even need to sign. Just start by enhancing your storytelling with body shifts, body mannerisms, appropriate facial expressions, and eye gazes. Soon, you will be taking a bow and doing an encore.

Using Signs in Storytelling

In this section you will learn common verbs. These general verbs are needed in storytelling and are easily applied in common everyday chatter.

▲ **COME:** Move both index fingers toward you in a beckoning motion. This sign is a natural gesture.

▲ **GO:** Move your index fingers away from your body. This sign is a natural gesture and can be moved in any direction.

◄ **TALK:** Use both extended index fingers, palms facing, moving back and forth from your mouth. To sign "conversation," use the handshape of "C," this is an "initialized" sign. *Variation:* To sign "yada, yada yada," move the "four" hand back and forth from the corner of your mouth.

◄ **RUN:** Use modified "L" hands. Hold your right thumb on your left index finger and move your hands forward quickly while flicking your right index finger and left thumb. *Memory aid:* This handshape is imitating a pair of feet, one in front of the other.

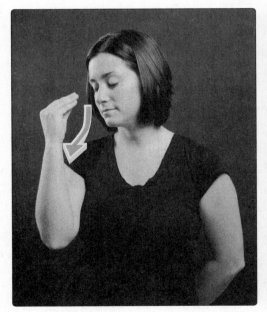

▲ **SLEEP:** With your palm facing inward, pull down while slowly closing your hand. Close your eyes and bend down your head.

▲ **WAKE UP:** Place both "G" hands at the corner of your closed eyes. Spread your index fingers and thumbs open, imitating eyes opening.

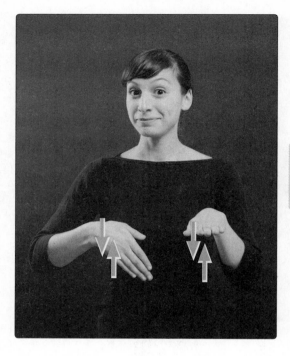

◀ **WALK:** Use the "flat" hands with palms facing down, and move your hands alternately, imitating walking.

This version is the natural gestural form. In Chapter 11, you will learn to use a "classifier" to demonstrate "walking," "running," "dancing," "jumping," and more.

You have just learned verbs. Some of these verbs are natural movements such as "come" and "go." Without thinking, you probably have already executed some of these signs in a natural gesture. The natural ease of forming and moving these signs is one of the elements that make sign language an attainable mode of communication.

The next sign is used frequently in signed conversations. It is the sign for "understand." This sign is presented in a question form and used as "understood" for affirmation. It is used and interjected during a long story or lengthy complicated conversation. Since sign language is a visual language, you can blink, sneeze, or break eye contact for a split second and miss a sign or two, or even three. Therefore, try to remember that applying this sign for "understand" is quite important.

▲ **UNDERSTAND:** Place the "S" hand at your temple, palm facing back, and then snap open your index finger to a vertical position.

Classifiers, the Powerful Tool

Now it's time to add yet another sign element to your new skills: classifiers. Classifiers give clarity, movement, and details without having to learn many new signs. Classifiers are specific handshapes with particular palm positions. The specific handshapes of classifiers can represent objects and display their movement, shapes, locations, and actions. Classifiers are a powerful tool when used in storytelling, they can provide a three-dimensional depth. When used correctly, classifiers add expediency and clarity to a signed conversation.

There are a vast number of classifiers. This chapter will just scratch the surface by presenting only seven basic handshapes of classifiers. Each of these seven classifiers has a specific name label, and that label can include an arrow or palm position instruction. When applying a classifier, the signer will use one or two hands as needed, in various palm positions.

The name labels of seven basic classifiers are derived from their handshapes:

- CL 3: Uses only "three" fingers, in various positions.
- CL 1: Uses the extended "one" finger, in various positions
- CL C: Uses the handshape of the letter "C," in various positions
- CL 5: Uses the handshape of a "claw" hand, in various positions
- CL Λ: Uses the letter "V," inverted and in various positions
- CL L: Uses the handshape of the letter "L," in various positions
- CL B: Uses letter "B" (flat hand), slightly modified, in various positions

These name labels are used in and throughout sign language dictionaries, books, and ASL courses. Classifiers can be formed in various positions; this is especially true when using the CL B, or flat hand.

Think of a classifier as pronoun. It can't be applied in a sentence until the signer explains what the classifier represents. Classifiers are not stand-alone nouns or verbs. Novice signers are taught to sign the object or noun first, before they apply the classifier. If a sign does not exist for an object, you can fingerspell the word, then set up, or apply the classifier handshape. Confused? Don't worry; following are a few examples to help you understand. You are already ahead of the learning curve, because some of these handshapes were demonstrated in Chapter 5.

The three-finger classifier (CL 3) is the easiest and most visual one to apply when relating a story or event. This CL 3 is used primarily when discussing a vehicle. You can think of this classifier as a minicar—one you can move all around. Form this classifier on both hands and you will have two cars. Move them around and you can describe a two-car collision. The index and middle fingertips are the front of your minicar. In Chapter 17, there is a detailed description of the three-finger classifier.

FACT

In 1699, George Dalgarno invented Dactylology. This method encouraged deaf students to wear a glove on the left hand. Vowels were written on the tips of the fingers and thumb, consonants were written on the palm. Using the right hand, the student would point to the letters spelling out words.

SIGNS FOR CLASSIFIERS

  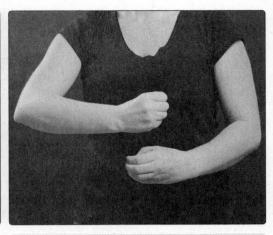

▲ **CLASSIFIER 3:** Extend your thumb, index finger, and middle finger. This classifier can represent cars, boats, trains, motorcycles, bicycles, and more.

▲ **CLASSIFIER 1:** Extend your index "one" finger. This classifier can represent thin long things, such as people, pencils, trees, sticks, poles, and lines.

▲ **CLASSIFIER C:** Form the handshape of the letter "C." This classifier can represent cylindrical items, such as a glass, cup, or bottle. *Note:* When you use two hands together in the shape of "C," you can make the shape of any vase, pipe, or cylindrical object with a gliding movement.

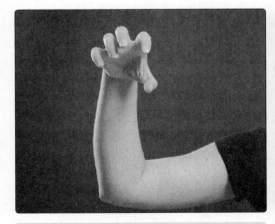 

▲ **CLASSIFIER 5:** Form a down-turned "claw" handshape. This classifier can represent a pile of laundry, a clump of hedges, or a mound of leaves.

▲ **CLASSIFIER Λ:** Form a letter "V" with your index and middle finger and turn it upside down. This classifier represents the "legs" of a person. Swinging the fingers back and forth can represent a person walking. *Variation:* Another extended form of a classifier is a "bent V." To form: Use the letter "V" with the index and middle fingers bent at the knuckles. Holding one or both hands slightly upright this classifier can be used to demonstrate animal movement, such as a rabbit hopping, frogs leaping, lions stalking, snakes slithering, and more.

SIGNS FOR CLASSIFIERS

CLASSIFIER L: Form the letter "L" with both hands, your thumb tips touching. This classifier can demonstrate small rectangular things such as licenses, license plates, bricks, checks, business cards, or credit cards. *Variation:* Another extended form of a classifier is using an "L" that is bent at the first knuckle. Place your two bent "L" hands together, thumb tips touching, and this classifier can demonstrate a small saucer. Spread your hands further apart, and you can shape out a large dinner plate or platter.

The next classifier is used frequently in describing multiple objects. It represents flat objects, such as papers, walls, floors, curtains, doors, tables, windows, ceilings, shelves, and more. By manipulating the position of the CL B, or "flat" hand classifier, you can make the shape of a box, which is also the shape of a room. The "flat" hand is the most commonly used hand-shape; not only does it work as a classifier, it is used extensively in forming signs.

ALERT!

The technical term for the "flat" hand classifier is "CL B." The handshape is actually a modified "B." It is modified in that the "thumb" is placed on the side of the hand, whereas in the manual alphabet, the letter "B" is formed with the thumb tucked into the palm.

Next, you will view five images of the various palm positions that can be used when applying the CL B. These images illustrate moving the "flat" handshape into various palm positions to demonstrate windows, walls, floors, curtains, and more.

SIGNS FOR CLASSIFIERS

The flat handshape is a powerful tool. Knowing how to move the "flat" hand classifier for visually specific information also makes it unique. This is especially true if you are redecorating and remodeling. The "flat" handshape is also a natural gesture. You have probably used this natural gesture many times when describing things, without giving it a second thought.

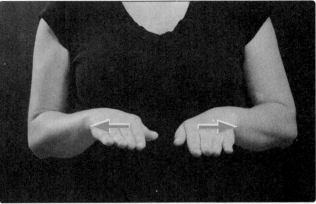

▲ **CLASSIFIER B** ↕ **:** Hold both "flat" hands edge to edge. The little finger of your right hand should rest on top of your left thumb, and your palms should face inward. Move your right hand up and down to demonstrate opening and closing a window.

▲ **CLASSIFIER B** ←→ **:** Hold both "flat" hands side by side, palms facing down. Separate your hands by sliding them apart. This handshape and movement demonstrates a tabletop, countertop, floor, or any basic horizontal flat surface.

REMEMBER: When the CL B, or flat handshape, is used to describe flat objects such as walls, windows, floors, or a room it is called a classifier.

▲ **CLASSIFIER B** ↓ ←→ **:** Hold both "flat" hands side by side vertically, palms facing forward. This handshape moved in various directions can demonstrate an array of doors such as a regular, sliding, or swinging double doors. Move the flat handshapes downward and they can represent drapes on a window and more.

SIGNS FOR CLASSIFIERS

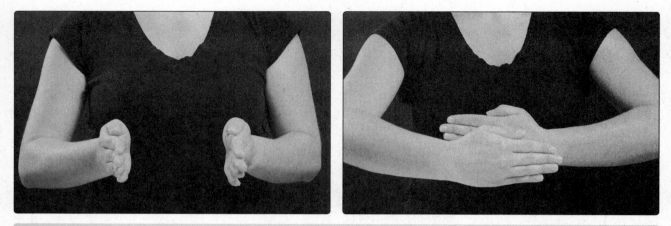

▲ **CLASSFIER B □:** Hold both "flat" hands facing each other in the first position (left image). Change to the second position, both palms facing inward with the left hand close to the body (right image). The palm positions and movements demonstrate first the sidewalls, then the front and back walls, forming a room. The movement demonstrates any item that is square, or box shaped.

Mold It, Shape It

This section will help you take a look at the different ways you can use those classifier handshapes. The following table shows a list of items beneath their appropriate classifier. These items can be easily pictured in your mind. Using classifiers, you can form these shapes as big or as small as you desire. You can move and arrange them anywhere within your signing space. Remember, some of these items require you to use two hands when shaping them with classifiers. Think of your hands as the tools for molding and shaping the objects. In a set of instructions, the abbreviation "CL" is used for classifiers.

CL B Flat hand	CL 5 Claw hand	CL C "C" hand	CL L Bent "L"	CL 1 "One" hand
Box	Snowball	Glass	Plate	Tree
Table	Light bulb	Flashlight	Pizza tray	Thermometer
Book	Flowerbed	Cup	Cookie	Stripes
Floor	Bushes	Bowl	Badge	Telephone pole
Window	Rubbish	Vacuum hose	Coaster	Person
Curtains	Laundry piles	Vase	Saucer	Popsicle

Remember, a sign for every word does not exist. Using classifiers fills the gaps and adds greater visual clarity. This short introduction to classifiers will give you a major advantage should you enroll in an ASL course. Don't worry about grasping all the concepts right now. The next chapter makes one of the classifiers much easier to understand by "letting your fingers do the walking."

CHAPTER 11

Ready, Set, Go!

It's time to play! In this chapter, you will learn how to apply a simple classifier to show physical movements, such as walking, sitting, and dancing. You will also be introduced to sports signs and learn how to transform them into compound signs. Remember, it's playtime, so have fun while you learn the subjects in this chapter.

Let Your Fingers Do the Walking

A signer can show many movements by simply moving the index and middle fingers into various positions. This handshape introduced in Chapter 10 is a classifier and the hand position is an upside down "V," and it is used to demonstrate movements or body positions. Here are common movement signs.

◀ **WALK:** Make an inverted "V" with your index and middle fingers and alternately swing the fingers, imitating walking.

◀ **STAND:** Use your index and middle fingers to make an inverted "V." Place the fingers onto your left open palm, imitating a pair of legs standing.

◀ **JUMP, HOP:** Place the inverted "V" onto the left open palm, then pull up while bending both fingers and knuckles, imitating jumping.

◀ **STAND ON ONE LEG:** Use the index and middle fingers to make an inverted "V," onto the left open palm, then pull up one finger.

◀ **KNEEL, CRAWL:** To sign "kneel," place the knuckles of the inverted "V" hand onto the left open palm. To sign "crawl," alternately move the knuckles forward, imitating the movement of crawling.

◀ **LIE DOWN:** Place the right "V" hand, palm down, onto your left open palm.

◀ **FALL:** Place the inverted "V" hand onto the left open palm. Now make the "V" jump off the end of your fingers, imitating falling. This is "fall" as in physically falling, and then there is a different sign for "fall" as in autumn.

◀ **DANCE:** Place the inverted "V" onto the open palm, swing your hand back and forth, and kick up your "heels."

The application of the inverted "V" classifiers, when used by nurses and medical professionals, is extremely helpful. These professionals are able to demonstrate to patients how they need to be positioned for physical therapy, procedures, tests, examinations, or for their comfort.

To sign "lie on side," place the right "V" hand onto your left palm, on the edge of either the index or middle finger, depending on which side you want to demonstrate.

To sign "roll over," place the right "V" hand, palm down, onto your left palm, then flip the "V" hand over. A cute way to demonstrate you "didn't sleep at all last night," is to make this movement several times, because you tossed and turned.

◀ **SIT:** Bend the knuckles of your right inverted "V" hand over your extended left "H" hand. Visualize legs dangling over the edge of a chair.

To sign "swing," form the sign for "sit," then swing your hands back and forth, imitating sitting on a swing.

Sport Signs

In this section, you will apply the "person" ending that was introduced in Chapter 9. This is a great chance to practice your newfound knowledge. The next set of vocabulary words will be related to sports. However, you can double that vocabulary set by simply signing the sport and then transforming it to indicate the player. For instance, if you sign the word "golf" then add the "person" sign, the sign becomes "golfer."

The following images of sport signs serve a dual purpose. From them, you will learn to sign specific sports, while at the same time you will continue to learn how to form a compound sign. As mentioned before, the compound sign is made by simply adding the "person" sign immediately after signing any one of these sports signs described. Just to refresh your memory, take another look at the "person" sign in Chapter 9.

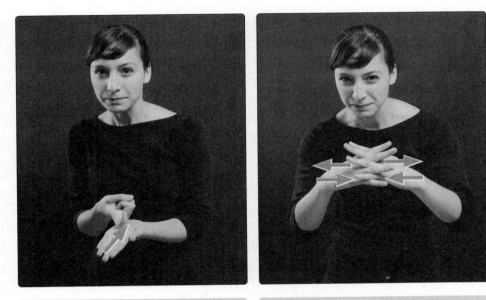

▲ **HOCKEY:** Use your bent index finger to sweep across the "open" left palm, imitating a hockey stick. Add the "person" sign, and the sign becomes "hockey player."

▲ **FOOTBALL:** Use both "open five" hands, palms facing each other, and interlock your fingers together several times, imitating two teams crashing together. Add the "person" sign, and now the sign becomes "football player."

FACT

The football huddle was invented by Paul D. Hubbard. Hubbard was a quarterback on the Gallaudet football team, and his opponents were deaf. The team learned that the opposing teams were reading their signed messages and could understand their team plays. Therefore, Hubbard decided to make a team huddle. This huddle is now a tactic used by all football teams.

As you can see, many of the sports signs are mimed or gestured. Here are a few more that are signed exactly the way you would imagine:

- To sign "baseball," hold both fists at shoulder level, imitating holding a baseball bat.
- To sign "golf," hold both fists as though you are swinging a golf club.
- To sign "swimming," move both arms, imitating a swimming stroke.
- To sign "basketball," hold an imaginary basketball and imitate the action of shooting a basket.

Add the "person" sign to each of the sports, and the sign describes a player of the sport (baseball player, golfer, swimmer, basketball player).

Additional Compound Signs

As you have seen, sports signs can be transformed to mean the players themselves by forming a compound sign. However, sports signs aren't the only ones you can use in compound signs. As your sign vocabulary grows, you will begin to recognize many of these types of compound signs. You have learned how easy it is to form a compound sign, which adds detail and clarity to the topic. Here are two more examples of using compound signs.

◀ **CAMERA:** Hold an imaginary camera up to the eye and press the shutter button with the index finger. Remember, adding the "person" sign changes this sign to "photographer."

◄ **PAINT:** To sign "paint," brush the right fingertips back and forth across the left "open" palm, imitating brush strokes. Add the "person" sign, and now the sign becomes "painter."

Play Ball!

A sports chapter in a sign language book would not be complete without a story about a famous deaf ballplayer. William Ellsworth "Dummy" Hoy was born in 1862. He lived to be nearly 100 years old before passing away in 1961. Hoy was the first deaf professional baseball player in the major leagues.

There are several stories surrounding Hoy and his contributions to the game of baseball. Some of these stories have been validated by old newspaper clippings from as far back as 1888. In the early days of baseball, all umpire calls were shouted. It is said Hoy was responsible for the creation of the signals for "strike," "safe," and "out." Hoy created these signals because neither he nor the crowd could hear the calls by the home plate umpires. Today these signals are tradition and are used by umpires worldwide.

FACT

Some say that the intricate system of hand signals used in baseball and softball games today can be traced back to Hoy. These additional signals would include the manager's call signals to the batter, as well as the outfielders' calls.

William Hoy was one of the few players to have played in four of the five recognized major leagues, and he held an outstanding baseball career record. The crowds loved Hoy, and to show their approval, they stood in the bleachers and waved their hats and arms to demonstrate their enthusiasm. Some say this is the first early form of "deaf applause," a visual form of applauding.

◀ **DEAF APPLAUSE:** Raise both hands high in the air, in an "open five" position, and shake them.

CHAPTER 12

Father Time

The subject of time is part of our everyday conversations. This chapter will introduce you to many of the common "time" signs. You will quickly learn the months of the year and their fingerspelled abbreviations. There will also be seasons and holiday signs to add to your new sign vocabulary.

Past, Present, and Future

There are a few easy-to-follow rules to use when signing units of time. These rules have been created to add clarity to a signed conversation. One of these rules governs when a signer should apply a "time" sign. The rule is simple: Always sign the time element *first* when relating a story or an event. For example, if you were describing last year's vacation you would sign "past year" first, then describe your vacation. In conversations using "now," "yesterday," and "tomorrow," the signer needs only to sign the time element once unless there is a change in the conversation of the time being discussed.

As you can see from the images, signs relating to the future are clearly indicated with a forward-moving arrow. The further you move your arm and hand forward, the further the date is in the future. In reverse, the same applies to signs relating to the past.

Now, try to imagine a physical timeline that goes straight through your body, extending out in front and back behind you. This imaginary line in front and back of you is there to represent the future and the past. All signs indicating the future are made in a forward movement and are out ahead of your body. Signs indicating the past are made with a backward movement and are pushed behind your shoulder. Therefore, the rule is: The future moves forward, and the past moves backward.

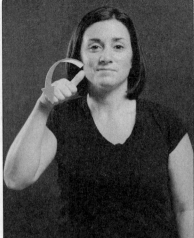

▲ **FUTURE:** Use the "flat" hand, palm facing left. Move it forward and down.

▲ **TOMORROW:** Use the "A" hand on your cheek, and turn it forward and down.

▲ **PAST:** Hold the "flat" hand palm inward and push it over your shoulder.

▲ **YESTERDAY:** Use the "Y" or modified "A" hand on your cheek and turn it backward.

▲ **NOW, PRESENT:** The "now" or "present" sign has two variations. It can also be formed using the "bent" or "Y" hands coming down in front and alongside the body. In the timeline, your body is the very center, indicating that you are standing in the "present/now" time. The sign used to indicate the "present" is formed just in front and alongside of your body.

Signing a Specific Time

Another way of indicating time is to simply point to your watch. When indicating a specific time, point to the watch, sign the number for the time, and then point again to the watch. To the receiver/reader, it would look like this: time, number, time. In Chapter 8, you learned how to form the signs for numbers. When indicating time on a clock or watch, you need to combine number signs. It is important to make sure that you learn and remember all of the basic signs for time, as they are used frequently in a signed conversation.

◄ **TIME:** Tap the top of the wrist twice, imitating tapping a watch.

◄ **MINUTE:** Place the "one" hand on your left-facing vertical palm. Move your index finger forward, imitating the hands ticking on a clock.

◀ **HOUR:** Place the "one" hand on your left-facing vertical palm. Rotate your index finger forward one turn, imitating one hour on the face of a clock.

General Times

The three general time signs—morning, noon, and night—are iconic in their compositions. The position of the arms for these signs relates closely to the sun's movements as it rises and sets. When holding your left arm stationary in front of you, imagine your arm to be the horizon. The sun comes peeking over the horizon in the morning. At noon, the sun shines down from directly overhead, and at night, the sun disappears again down below the horizon.

◀ **DAY:** Hold your right arm vertical, palm facing left. Rest your right elbow on the back of the fingertips of your left arm. Bring the right arm slowly down to rest on the left arm. *Variation:* This sign can be made with either the "flat" hand or the "D" hand.

To sign "morning," hold your left arm horizontal and move your right "flat" hand up slightly, palm inward, in front of your left arm. Visualize the sun rising up over the horizon. "Noon" or "afternoon" is signed this way: hold your right arm vertical, "flat" hand palm forward. Rest your right elbow on the back of the fingertips of your left arm. And finally, to sign "night" or "evening," hold your left arm horizontal. Move your right "flat" hand over and down slightly, palm inward, in front of your left arm. Visualize the sun going down into the horizon.

◄ **LATE, NOT YET:** Place the "flat" hand near your waist, palm facing back, and push back.

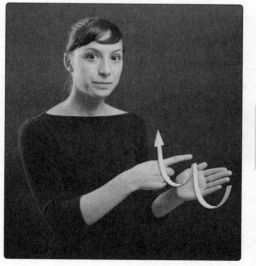

◄ **ONCE IN AWHILE, SOMETIMES:** To sign "once in awhile" or "sometimes," swipe the index finger of your "one" hand on your left palm twice.

◄ **YEAR:** Circle your right "S" hand forward and around your left "S" hand, and rest it on the top of your left hand.

◄ **NEVER:** Move the "flat" hand, palm facing left, in a downward movement in the shape of a question mark.

Learning the Calendar

Using the alphabet, fingerspell the months of the year. Each month has an abbreviation. The abbreviated form is the preferred way when used in a signed conversation. Your signing skills will be strengthened when you see these abbreviations as a whole word. Seeing an abbreviated sign as a whole sign means you aren't looking to read each letter, but rather you are seeing the shape of the whole sign. This skill is an important part of beginning to recognize initialized and loan signs. It is a skill that takes time to master and that will require patience on your part. Here are a few practice tips. Look at the shape that the abbreviation creates rather than the individual letters. Remember to do your hand warm-ups before you fingerspell.

Abbreviation	Word	Abbreviation	Word
J-A-N	January	J-U-L	July
F-E-B	February	A-U-G	August
M-A-R	March	S-E-P-T	September
A-P-R	April	O-C-T	October
M-A-Y	May	N-O-V	November
J-U-N	June	D-E-C	December

Variation: Any month that has five letters or less can be fingerspelled in its entirety.

The next thing to learn is the days of the week. Once again, you will borrow from the alphabet and "initialize" nearly all the days of the week. There are three well-known variations, which are only in the movement, that are the result of regional and geographical differences. Here are the different ways these signs are made:

◄ **MONDAY—**
FIRST VARIATION: The palm is facing you and your arm moves in a small circle, as if swinging a lasso.

◄ **MONDAY—**
SECOND VARIATION: The palm is facing you and your arm moves in a small circle, counterclockwise.

◄ **MONDAY—**
THIRD VARIATION: The palm faces the reader/receiver and moves in a clockwise motion.

These three variations are used throughout the country, and it is best that you are familiar with all three. However, following the rules of finger-spelling, which says the palm must face the reader/receiver, the chart on the following page gives you instructions for the *third* variation.

Day	Sign Direction
Monday	Use the "M" hand, and rotate in a small clockwise circle.
Tuesday	Use the "T" hand, and rotate in a small clockwise circle.
Wednesday	Use the "W" hand, and rotate in a small clockwise circle.
Thursday	Use the "H" hand, and rotate in a small clockwise circle.
Friday	Use the "F" hand, and rotate in a small clockwise circle.
Saturday	Use the "S" hand, and rotate in a small clockwise circle.

Signing "Sunday" is a little different.

◀ **SUNDAY:** Use the "open five" hands, with your palms forward, move your hands in opposite circular motions.

It is easy to remember how to sign the days of the week because you are simply initializing the first letter. There are only two exceptions. Thursday uses the letter "H" because we have already used "T" for Tuesday, and Sunday is not an initialized sign at all. Instead, the sign represents a "wonderful" day.

E ALERT!

A signer needs to respect the variations in signs. This is especially true when seeing and using any of the "time" signs. There are thirteen different ways to sign Sunday; three for Monday, Tuesday, Wednesday, and Friday; four for Saturday; and five for Thursday.

Time to Celebrate

In this section, you will learn how to sign the seasons, as well as a few of the holidays appropriate to the seasons. Visualizing seasonal changes that occur in nature will help you memorize how to form the signs for the seasons. For instance, during the summer it is very hot, so visualize what happens when you are perspiring. You need to wipe the sweat off your brow when forming this sign. During the winter, you are feeling cold and shivering. In springtime, the flowers push up through the ground to bloom, and fall brings the leaves floating down to the ground. The images that follow resemble these descriptions.

▲ **SUMMER:** Use a "bent" index finger and drag it across the forehead.

▲ **WINTER:** Shake the "S" hands while holding your arms against the body and imitate shivering. *Memory aid:* It is cold outside, and this makes you shiver. Think of feeling cold when forming this sign. This sign is also used for "cold." *Variation:* Another way to sign winter is to shake the "W" hands in the same manner while shivering.

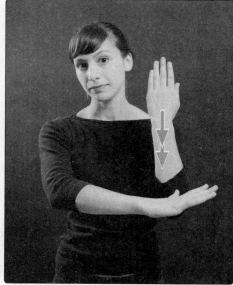

▲ **SPRING, GROW:** Push your right hand up through the "open" left hand. This sign represents the growth that occurs during spring.

▲ **FALL, AUTUMN:** Hold your left arm out, slightly tilted to the right, palm facing inward. Stroke the right slightly "open-five" hand down along the left forearm to the elbow, imitating leaves tumbling or a barren tree.

◄ **FALL—VARIATION:** Use both "open five" hands, palms facing down. Start high, and float your "open five" hands side to side while moving downward, imitating leaves falling.

Valentine's Day is one of the special days celebrated in many different fashions. You have already learned the "I love you" sign, and the sign for "love." Now you have two ways to say "love" to your significant other on Valentine's Day.

▲ **VALENTINE'S DAY:** Use both "V" hands to outline the shape of your heart on your chest. This is an initialized sign.

▲ **THANKSGIVING:** Bring the fingertips of the right and left "flat" hands from the lip area with a double forward movement. This sign is derived from the sign for "thank you" which has only one forward movement.

◄ **HANUKKAH:** Position the "four" hands side by side with palms facing you. Separate both hands simultaneously to the sides in a small upward arc. This represents the eight lit candles of the menorah. *Variation:* Position the "four" hands side by side with palms facing forward. Separate both hands simultaneously to the sides in a small upward arc.

Sign Variations

As you have learned, signs can be formed in more than one way and have various representations. These variations occur for several reasons—regional, geographical, the result of progress and technology, and at times, cultural or religious reasons. This chapter is a small representation of the many variations of signs within this visual language.

For example, the sign for Christmas has twelve variations, and the sign for Santa has fifteen. The sign you would select to represent Christmas or Santa may depend on where you live as well as on your specific beliefs.

- **Christmas:** Form an arcing "C" that moves left to right in front of the body, representing half a wreath.
- **Christmas Tree:** First form the sign for Christmas then using both "flat" hands mime the shape of a Christmas tree.
- **Santa Claus:** Form Santa's large imaginary beard with both "C" hands, then move both hands downward to mime Santa's large belly.

◄ **SANTA:** Using both "curved five" hands, mime Santa's large beard.

A good signer should always stay flexible and understand there will always be differences within ASL. Additionally, a good signer is one who learns many variations of a sign, and is familiar with a wide range of choices in forming signs.

CHAPTER 13

The Great Outdoors

The great outdoors offers a perfect sign language lesson. You can go for a walk, and while enjoying the fresh air you can see and practice what you have just learned. This chapter will introduce you to the signs for different animals, weather, and some of nature's finest elements.

A Word about Service Dogs

When the subject of animals comes up, one cannot omit the wonderful work of service animals. These animals are service dogs, guide dogs, hearing dogs, social dogs, and many other types of specially trained dogs. They provide assistance to many different types of individuals, such as the blind, deaf, physically challenged, and more.

ESSENTIAL

The bonding of personalities between a service dog and a human partner is the key factor in creating a successful, and often lifelong, partnership. Finding and training the right dog to the right human partner often takes a year or more.

The hearing ear service dog, (signal dog) is specially trained for the deaf and hard of hearing. Hearing dogs alert their owners to a variety of sounds. Here are examples of some of the sounds hearing dogs are trained to differentiate and alert their partners to: the sound of their partner's name being called, a knock on the door, doorbells, alarm clocks, phones, a baby crying, various electronic signaling devices, smoke and fire alarms, and sounds of food boiling over on a stove. When a sound occurs, the hearing dog will locate the sound and make a determination. The dog will then either sit in a certain place for his partner to make a further determination or pull his partner to safety. Service dogs also alert their partners through their body language, such as the turn of their head or position of their ears.

Have you ever stepped out into a busy parking lot and moved quickly out of harm's way because you heard a vehicle approaching? The hearing dog is trained to alert his partner to just such a danger. The hearing dog's main responsibility is to make sure his partner is safe by acting as his partner's ears. The peace of mind and assistance hearing dogs bring to their partners, such as the hard of hearing, the deaf, and late-deafened adults is invaluable and difficult to measure.

Service Dog Manners

At any time, in a public place or on a college campus you may see a service dog and a partner. Keep in mind, you are looking at a working team, and all disabilities are not visible. It is important to understand a service dog is *not a pet*. When these dogs are "dressed," meaning wearing their special collars, coats (usually of a bright orange color), harnesses, and identifications, they are working. In order to assist and provide for the needs of their partners, service dogs need to maintain their full concentration. The best approach during an encounter with a service dog is to completely ignore them and allow them to do their work.

FACT

Hearing ear service dogs and their partners have full rights under the American Disabilities Act (ADA) to enter into all places of business. The Air Carrier Access Act of 1986 (ACAA) also protects the rights of disabled people by allowing their service dogs to enter airports and planes as regular passengers. Therefore, these valuable service dogs are not placed in carriers or in cargo holds.

In the event of an encounter, here is a list of service dog manners or rules of etiquette:

- Never touch a service dog or its partner. This could be interpreted as an assault.
- Do not make distracting sounds toward a service dog.
- Never offer food to a service dog.
- Never allow children to approach or play with a service dog.
- Never interfere with a working service dog and partner.
- Do not ask personal questions about one's disability.

These etiquette rules, and service dog manners may sound strict. However, they are in place to protect you, the service dog, and its partner. Though you may be curious about a service dog, do not be offended if a person does not wish to chat. He may not have a lot of time to answer questions or a desire to share personal information. Service dogs are trained to ignore distractions. Why make their job more difficult? Remember, you should simply ignore a service dog in a public place. Lastly, it is important to teach children about those who have disabilities, and the valuable work of service dogs.

To sign "dog," snap the "D" hand into the "G" hand waist high and out to your side. This sign represents your dog being obedient and heeling at your side. When signing "dog" to children simple pat your side twice, do not snap your fingers. Adult signers sign "D to G" *or* pat their side, however, signing both is considered redundant.

The Menagerie

Animal signs are a delight to learn, as they are often iconic. In this chapter, you have the opportunity to apply the classifiers that you have just learned and combine them with this new group of sign vocabulary. After studying the new vocabulary, you will be able to use classifiers as an enhancer, giving you a wonderful way to show movement. As an example, you can combine the classifier for animal movement (a bent "V" hand) with the animal sign for "lion." This combination of a classifier and a sign demonstrates that the lion is moving. When you use this classifier slowly, you can suggest the appearance of a lion crouching. Add the sign for "tree," which you will also find in this chapter. Now, simply pluralize tree by signing it multiple times. Voila! You have just added a jungle.

ESSENTIAL

Children love animal signs. The following is a fun variation for "bunny:" Place your thumbs on either side of your head, fingers together and bent downward. This handshape represents a bunny with floppy ears.

▲ **ANIMAL:** Place the fingertips of both hands on your chest and rock the hands back and forth, imitating an animal breathing.

▲ **LION:** Pull the "claw" hand back over your head, imitating a lion's enormous mane.

◄ **TIGER:** Use both "claw" hands placed on both sides of your cheeks and draw them apart several times, imitating a tiger's stripes.

◄ **RABBIT:** Place the "three" hands on both sides of your head, palms facing back. Flick your fingers and thumb repeatedly, imitating the ears. The "flat" hand held in the same position can be used for very young children. *Variation:* Use the "H" hands, cross wrists, palms facing in, in front of your chest. Flick your fingers repeatedly.

▲ **BEAR:** Use "claw" hands and cross your arms on your chest, moving the hands to imitate clawing.

▲ **CAT:** Pull both "F" hands from the corners of your mouth to the sides, imitating a cat's whiskers.

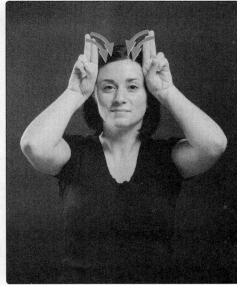

▲ **COW:** Place the thumb of both "Y" hands at your temple and twist, imitating the cow's horns. Good signers use two hands for children which adds strong visuals to stories and use just one hand with adults *Note:* Make this sign with two hands and it will add animation.

▲ **HORSE:** Place the "H" hands, palms forward, on your head and flick your fingers.

◄ **BIRD:** Open and close your index finger and thumb at the side of your mouth, representing a small beak.

NOTE: Signing bird, duck, and goose can be an adventure in learning sizes for a young child. Sign a small beak for a bird, medium beak for duck, and a large beak for goose. To sign "duck," open and close your index finger, middle finger, and thumb at the side of your mouth, representing a medium-size beak. To sign "goose," open and close your thumb and all fingers at the side of your mouth, representing a large beak.

▲ **SKUNK:** Place the "K" hand at the bridge of your nose and pull back over your head, imitating the white stripe on a skunk.

▲ **WOLF:** Place a slightly open hand over your nose and pull down, while closing your hand, to the end, imitating the long nose of a wolf.

◄ **RACCOON:** Place both "V" hands, palms inward, at your eyes, and pull out to the sides, closing your fingers, imitating the mask of a raccoon.

◄ **DEER:** Place the thumbs of both "open five" hands at your temples, imitating antlers. To sign "moose," make the sign for "deer" and pull out the "open five" hands away from the side of the head, imitating the large antlers on a moose.

NOTE: When you are out on nature walks, there is a possibility that you might be carrying a pair of binoculars. The sign for "binoculars" is a natural, gestural sign; just place both "O" hands on the eyes and twist back and forth. When you form the sign for "binoculars," you also are signing "owl."

▲ **SQUIRREL/CHIPMUNK:** Use both "bent V" hands, palms facing together. Tap fingertips and knuckles multiple times, imitating the squirrel's gnawing.

▲ **SNAKE:** To sign "snake," move the bent "V" hand forward in a winding movement, imitating a snake.

◀ **DINOSAUR:** Hold your right arm vertical, palm facing left. Rest your elbow on the back of the fingertips of your left horizontal arm. Use the flattened "O" hand and pivot your wrist back and forth slowly, imitating the swaying head of a dinosaur.

▲ **FROG:** Place your closed fist under your chin, flick open your index and middle fingers, imitating the frog's throat.

▲ **BUG:** Place the tip of your thumb on the tip of your nose and wiggle the bent index and middle fingers, imitating antennae on a bug.

▲ **SPIDER:** To sign "spider," cross both "open five" hands at the wrist and wiggle your fingers while moving forward, imitating a spider crawling.

▲ **TURTLE:** Place the "A" hand, palm facing left, under the "curved" left hand. Move the thumb of your "A" hand back and forth under the left curved hand, imitating the head of a turtle inside its shell.

To sign "sea turtle," place the right fist on top of the left fist and extend both thumbs. Rotate both thumbs simultaneously, imitating a sea turtle swimming.

To sign "manta ray," place the right "flat" hand on top of the left "flat" hand, extend thumbs and move them back and forth, while moving hands forward in a slight wavy motion.

The Weatherman

The morning news comes on, and the weatherman announces it is going to be cold today. There will be rain with lightning and thunder. There is even a possibility of the weather changing to snow. A family member is flying out the door, and you want to warn her of the change in the weather pattern.

In just a moment, you will be able to sign this from the doorway as she is getting in the car. The added communication benefits that come with long-distance signing are yet another great reason to learn sign language.

▲ **WEATHER:** Use the "W" hands, palms facing. Twist your hands in opposite directions twice. This sign represents the ever-changing weather patterns.

▲ **CLOUD, FOG:** Make a swirling motion with both "claw" hands above your head for "cloud." The sign for "fog" is similar to the "cloud" sign, except it's formed about waist high. This makes perfect sense: clouds are in the sky, and fog is near the ground.

NOTE: In Chapter 3 you were introduced to the sign for "rain." You can change "rain" to "snow" just by wiggling your fingers.

◄ **SNOW:** Wiggle the fingers of the "open five" hands, dropping your hands down several times, imitating falling snowflakes.

◄ **THUNDER:** Tap both "A" hands alternately against your chest. You can feel the rumble in your body.

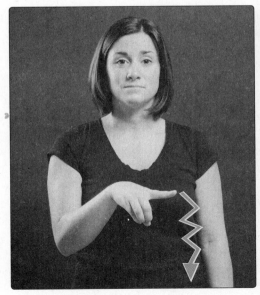

▲ **LIGHTNING:** Use your index finger and trace a downward zigzag movement, imitating a lightning bolt.

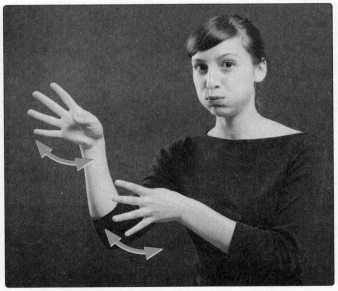

▲ **WIND, BREEZE:** Sweep the "open five" hands side to side in front of your body. The intensity with which you move your hands back and forth in front of your body will indicate the wind's gentleness or its ferocity.

▲ **SUN:** Use your index finger and form a clockwise circle above the right side of your head. *Variation:* To sign "sunshine," sign "sun," then form a wide "open five" to show the rays of the sun.

▲ **SKY:** Using both "flat" hands, palms facing, cross your arms in front of your body above your head in an arched movement and spread your arms open. *Variation:* This sign can be formed using one "curved" hand forming a large arc from left to right above the head.

Nature's Best

Nature's vast and wonderful world is filled with amazing creatures and natural beauty. Sign language, with its iconic elements, reflects some of this beauty. If you are a nature lover or photographer, or if you just like to walk in the woods, you will appreciate these signs.

E-QUESTION

What is Usher's syndrome?
Usher's syndrome is a hereditary condition that results in the loss of eyesight and hearing. This condition represents 10 percent of all hereditary deafness and affects 3 babies out of every 1 million. People with Usher's syndrome use "tactile signing." This form of sign language relies on the sense of touch to be understood.

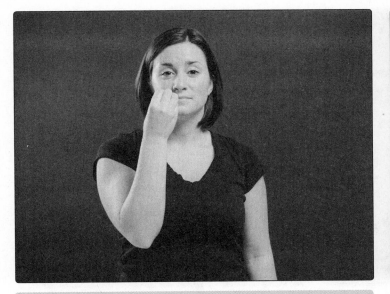

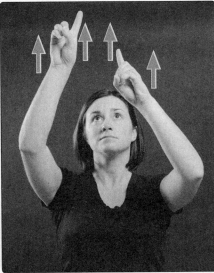

▲ **FLOWER:** Gently tap the "O" hand under your right nostril and then the left. This sign and movement imitates smelling flowers. Form this sign with an "R" hand and you are signing "Rose."

▲ **STARS:** Point both index fingers upward and move your fingers alternately skyward.

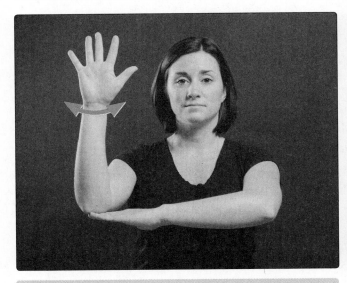

▲ **TREE:** Hold your right arm vertical and rest the elbow on the back of the fingertips of the hand of the left horizontal arm. Using an "open five" hand, palm facing forward, pivot your wrist back and forth repeatedly. *Note:* To form "forest/jungle" repeat the formation while moving the arm right to left, imitating many trees.

▲ **RAINBOW:** Hold the left "four" hand vertical, then sweep your right "four" hand left to right in an arc above your head, demonstrating the colors and shape in the sky.

▲ **OCEAN:** Move both your "curved" hands forward, palms down, with one hand slightly behind the other, imitating rolling waves on the ocean.

▲ **BEACH:** Begin with your elbow resting on the back of your left hand, held in front of the body. Brush the outside edge of your left arm with your "flat" right hand several times.

This sign for "beach" allows the signer to show gentle or ferocious surf. This sign can also demonstrate high tide by sweeping the right hand high above the arm or low tide by sweeping outward and down below the arm.

In this chapter, there have been many beautiful signs. Explore putting together signs to create short sentences. Your sign vocabulary is building. Signs from Chapter 7 would help create sentences, such as "The sky is beautiful." "I am happy to see the sun." Keep in mind, small words such as "the" and "is" do not need to be signed.

CHAPTER 14

Let the Banquet Begin

Cooking and eating are two of America's favorite activities. In this chapter, the signs for foods and related items are bountiful. It is here that you will learn to make the signs for some of your favorite foods. So, let the banquet begin!

Don't Skip Breakfast

It's time to eat. You need to look at food selections and plan the menu for the day. You can start with breakfast, then move on to lunch, dinner, and, of course, dessert. Along with learning the signs for foods, signs are also presented for cooking techniques and for the other items found in the kitchen.

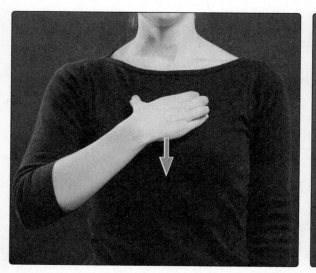

▲ **HUNGRY:** Draw the "C" hand down the center of your chest once, imitating a hollow feeling. *Note:* This sign is also used for the interpersonal sign of "desire."

▲ **FOOD, EAT:** To sign "food," tap your lips with the modified "O" hand in a bouncy movement, imitating eating. To sign "eat," do the same but with a much more steady movement.

You learned in Chapter 12 how to make the various signs that represent time. In this chapter, you will combine these time signs with other signs. Take a moment and review how to form "morning," "noon/afternoon," and "evening/night." In the *morning*, a person *eats* breakfast, and this is exactly the description in ASL. To sign "breakfast" first sign "morning" and continue to move your hand up to the lips to sign "eat." Or, gently tap your chin with the side of your "B" hand facing left. This version is an initialized sign.

The day gets off to a better start with a good breakfast. Would you like to have bacon and eggs? These menu selections can be served with toast, a little jam or jelly, and a banana. Of course, what would the morning be without coffee and orange juice? Here are the signs for these breakfast selections:

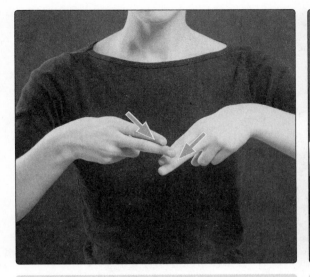

▲ **EGGS:** Strike the edges of both "H" hands together, then slightly spread them apart, imitating breaking an egg.

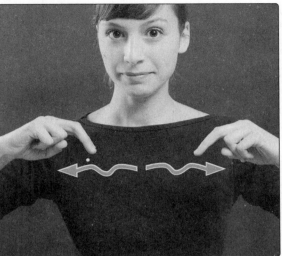

▲ **BACON:** To sign "bacon," touch the tips of both "U" hands, palms down, and draw them apart with a wiggle, imitating bacon sizzling in a pan.

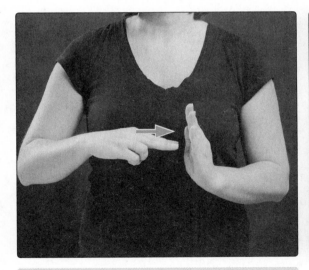

▲ **TOAST:** Hold the left "flat" hand, palm facing right. Tap the right "V" hand into your palm, and on the back of your left hand. *Visualize:* You are toasting both the top and bottom of a slice of bread by tapping the "V" on *both* side of the "flat" hand.

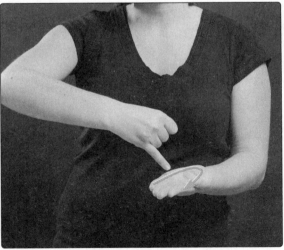

▲ **JAM, JELLY:** Trace the letter "J" into the left "open" palm, imitating spreading jelly.

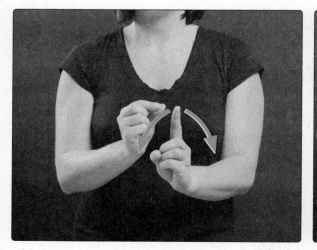

▲ **BANANA:** Hold your left index finger upright and use your right hand to imitate the motion of peeling a banana.

▲ **COFFEE:** Form the handshape of "C" with left hand, and rotate the right "S" hand counterclockwise above the left hand. Visualize turning the handle of a coffee grinder above your imaginary cup.

Chapter 7 demonstrated the color of "orange" by squeezing an "O" on your cheek. To sign "orange juice" make a very small modification: squeeze the "S" hand near the corner of your mouth or in front of your mouth.

Lunchtime!

Now it's time to learn the foods you eat at lunch. "Lunch" is signed in the same manner that you just signed "breakfast." To sign "lunch," form the sign for "noon" and then sign "eat." A variation would be to gently tap the mouth using the "L" hand. This version is an initialized sign.

For lunch you could have a few light selections, such as soup and a sandwich, or a nice healthy salad with a cold glass of milk.

But then again, you could always slip away to one of those fast-food restaurants! To sign "restaurant" tap the "R" hand once on each corner of your mouth. Here, you could order a mouthwatering hamburger with cheese, tomato, onion, and mayonnaise, and a large soda. Of course, you will also have to have that extra-large order of French fries.

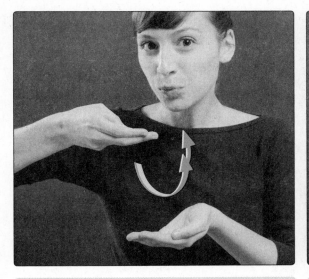

▲ **SOUP:** Scoop the right "H" hand, curved like a spoon, into the curved left palm. Bring your right hand a few times up to your mouth. Visualize holding a bowl in your left hand while your right hand acts as your spoon.

▲ **SANDWICH:** Bring the "flat" hands, palm-to-palm, toward your mouth, imitating eating a sandwich.

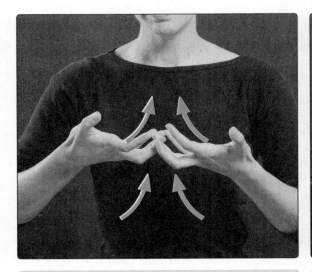

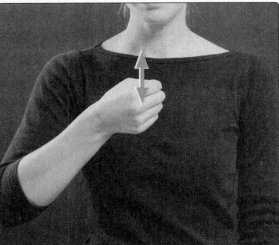

▲ **SALAD:** Move both "claw" hands, palms facing upward, and imitate tossing a salad in a bowl with your hands.

▲ **MILK:** Squeeze one or both "S" hands alternately up and down imitating milking a cow. Often, this sign is formed using just one hand.

"Hamburger" is a natural sign that imitates making a patty. Clasp both "curved" hands, as if you were making a patty, and then reverse direction.

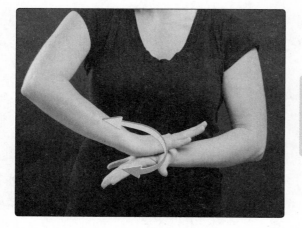

◄ **CHEESE:** Press the heels of both hands together, twisting back and forth, imitating pressing cheese.

When signing condiments or dressings that are spread on bread or rolls, you form the sign by imitating a spreading motion, on the "flat" palm drawn toward you. You need only to change the handshapes for the specific item.

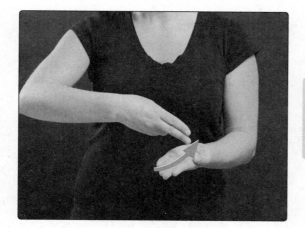

◄ **BUTTER:** Draw the extended fingers of the right "N" hand across the left "open" palm, imitating spreading butter.

- To sign "mayonnaise," draw the extended fingers of the "M" hand across your left "open" palm, imitating spreading mayonnaise.
- To sign "mustard," circle the extended fingers of the "M" hand on your left "open" palm, imitating squirting mustard on bread.
- To sign "French fries," slide the "F" hand to the right in two small movements in the fingerspelling position.

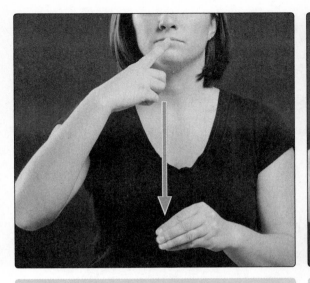

▲ **TOMATO:** First sign "red," then use your right index finger to strike the left fingertips of the modified "O" hand. *Note:* This is a compound sign. Visualize holding a tomato and slicing it.

▲ **ONION:** Twist the knuckle of the "X" hand in the corner of your eye. *Visualize:* Onions make you cry.

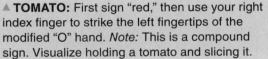

▲ **KETCHUP:** With your left "C" hand, hold an imaginary "ketchup" bottle upside down. Strike the bottom of the "bottle" with the heel of the right "open five" hand. *Variation:* Shake the "K" hand up and down. This version is an initialized sign, and one of many ways to sign "ketchup."

▲ **SODA:** Hold an imaginary can in your left hand and hit the top of the "can" with your right hand, imitating a "pop" sound. *Variation:* Holding the imaginary can with the left hand, the right middle finger is pushed into it, and then the hand hits the top. Another variation is to pull the ring before the hand hits the top of the can.

Afternoon Snack

You deserve a little break. It's time for tea, cookies, or fruit. On the other hand, perhaps you want a piece of candy!

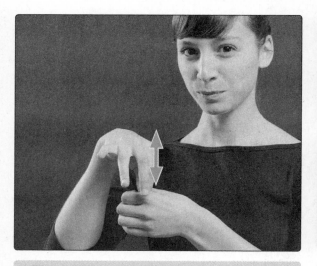

▲ **TEA:** Hold an imaginary cup with your left hand and dip the "F" hand in and out, imitating dipping a tea bag.

▲ **COOKIE:** Twist the "C" hand's fingertips back and forth on your left "open" palm, imitating cutting out cookies.

▲ **FRUIT:** To sign "fruit" twist the "F" hand near the corner of your mouth.

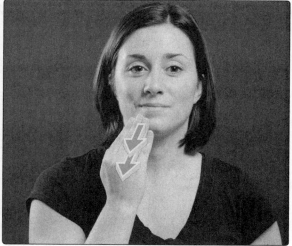

▲ **SWEET:** Brush the fingertips of your "flat" hand downward from the corner of your mouth and chin several times.

- To sign "sugar" or "candy," brush the fingertips of your "U" hand downward from the corner of your mouth and chin several times.
- The sign for "cute" is formed by brushing the fingertips of the "U" hand downward on the chin, with added expression.

Take a few minutes to review the signs before making a meal or setting the table. Then, just before you handle that item, see if you can remember how to sign it.

The Evening Meal

It is time for dinner. Perhaps this evening you will stay in and cook. You'll go into the kitchen, look inside the refrigerator, and see what there is to eat. It appears the selections for dinner are meat, baked potato, and fish. Then again, it would be simple to just boil some spaghetti, and serve it with bread and butter. In the meantime, while dinner is cooking, you'll set the table.

ALERT!

Daily practice is very important! One of the ways you can keep up with a daily practice routine is to fingerspell or sign your grocery list items before you write them down. Remember to include brand names in your practice.

To sign "dinner" or "supper," form the signs "night" and "eat." Together they create the sign. Variations: To sign "dinner," gently tap your mouth using the "D" hand. To sign "supper," gently tap your mouth using the "S" hand. These versions are initialized signs.

To sign "kitchen," flip the "K" hand back and forth on the palm of your stationary left hand. This version is an initialized sign.

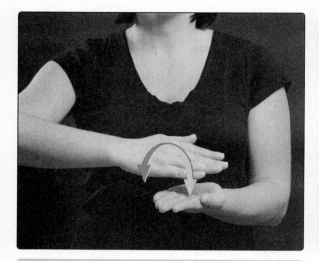

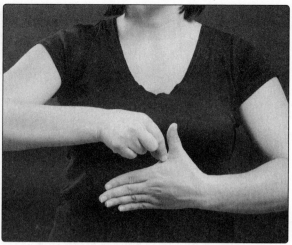

▲ **COOK:** To sign "cook," flip the "flat" hand back and forth on the palm of your stationary left hand.

▲ **MEAT:** Use your index finger and thumb to pinch the meaty part of your left hand between your thumb and index finger.

▲ **OVEN, BAKE:** Slide the "flat" hand, palm down, under the left "flat" hand, imitating sliding a pan into an oven.

▲ **POTATOES:** Tap the curved "V" hand on the back of your left fist, imitating piercing a baked potato.

▲ **FISH:** Move your extended arm, palm facing left, forward in a wiggling motion, imitating a swimming fish.

Spaghetti is a fun sign to form, and one that people seem to remember. The sign imitates how pasta looks when it comes out of a pasta maker. However, you can't eat the pasta until you boil the water (see facing page).

▲ **BOIL:** Wiggle the fingers of your right "curved five" hand under your left palm, imitating the heat under the pan bringing it to a boil.

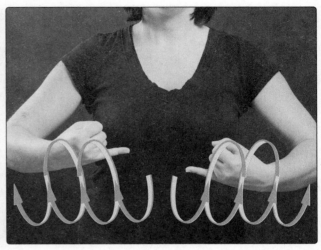

▲ **SPAGHETTI:** Touch the fingertips of both "I" hands together and pull them apart while forming a circular, curly motion.

▲ **BREAD:** Move the edge of your "flat" hand up and down on the back of your left hand, imitating slicing bread.

▲ **SALT:** Tap your extended index and middle fingers of your right hand on the extended index and middle fingers of your left hand.

PEPPER: Imitate holding a peppershaker and shake gently.

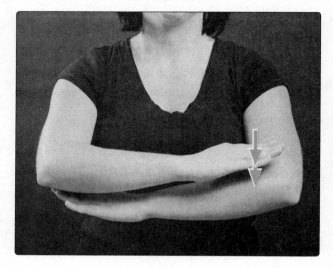

◀ **TABLE:** Place both arms across the front of your body, right on top of left, palms facing down, and tap your right palm to your left elbow, imitating a tabletop.

The "table" shown in this image is the one that is used to imply that things are set up on the "table," such as plates and cups.

FACT

Another sign for "table" is in Chapter 15, which demonstrates the simple structure of a table. Don't get confused. The image in this chapter is the correct image to use when you are talking about "food on the table."

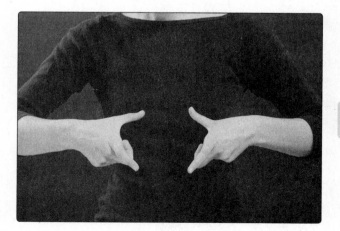

◀ **PLATE:** Hold both bent "L" hands together.

To sign "bowl," use both "C" hands. The size of the plate or bowl is indicated by how close or far apart the hands are held.

Next, you will need to draw on your memory. The next few signs are mimed or use the handshapes of signs that have previously been shown.

- **"Napkin":** Use your "flat" hand and mime dabbing or wiping your mouth with a napkin.
- **"Spoon":** Scoop your right "H" hand, curved like a spoon, into your curved left palm. This sign is formed the same as "soup," but you do not bring it toward your mouth.
- **"Fork":** Jab the inverted "V" into your "flat" left hand.
- **"Cup"/"Glass":** Use the handshape of "C."
- **"Water":** Tap the "W" hand on the lips, chin, or corner of your mouth.
- **"Wine":** Circle the "W" hand near the corner of your mouth in a backward motion.
- **"Beer":** Move the "B" hand in a backward motion twice near the corner of your mouth.

Sweet Temptations

A dessert is a delicious reward when you finish your meat and potatoes, and you've certainly earned such a treat after the meat and potatoes of this chapter! The selections from the dessert menu are cake, pie, and ice cream.

◀ **DESSERT:** Touch the fingertips of your "D" hands several times.

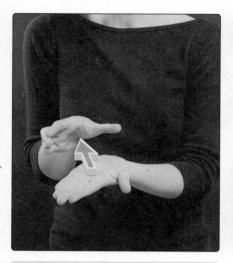

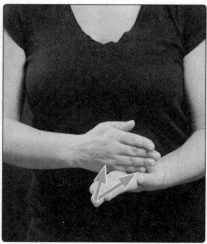

▲ **CAKE:** Pull the "C" hand across your left "open" palm, imitating pulling out a slice of cake.

▲ **PIE:** Use your "flat" hand to slice an imaginary piece of pie in your left "open" palm.

▲ **CHOCOLATE:** Circle the "C" hand on the back of your left hand.

To sign "vanilla" circle the "V" hand on the back of the left hand.

The sign for ice cream is fully mimed. As a child, there is a good chance that you mimed this sign before you attained your verbal skills. All you need to do is hold the cone and lick your imaginary ice cream.

ESSENTIAL

In order to keep these food signs fresh and clear in your memory, sign them every chance you get. Try to remember the importance of practice. The next time you sit down for a meal, sign, sign, and sign everything you see on the table.

Imagine it is the end of the day and you are planning to unwind. Pop some popcorn, and pour yourself a drink before you settle in front of the television for a while. To sign "TV," fingerspell the letters "T" and "V." This makes the "loan" sign for "television/TV." To sign "thirsty" stroke your index finger down the outside of your throat. To form the sign for a drink of Seven-Up, first sign the number "7," then with your index finger, point upward.

Form this combination of these two signs as smoothly as possible. Learning to combine and execute two or more signs smoothly gets you well underway to becoming a good signer.

◀ **POPCORN:** Flick both index fingers alternately, imitating popping corn. *Memory aid:* The flicking fingers imitate how popcorn appears when it is "popping."

Learning all these food items has probably made you hungry. Do you remember how to sign "hungry"? If you answered yes, good for you; it was the first sign in this chapter!

Keep up the good work!

CHAPTER 15

Around and About

Look around the living room at home and you will probably see a wide-screen TV and some type of telephone—two things that are taken for granted in most homes. In this chapter, you will look into learning how to sign items around the house and at work, and you will learn a little bit more about communication equipment for the deaf and hard of hearing.

Home Sweet Home

American Sign Language is really all about describing. When it comes to describing things around the house, there is one particular handshape that is used repeatedly—the "flat" hand. You were introduced to the "flat" hand, with the thumb neatly tucked at the side of the hand, (also known as the modified "B") in Chapter 10. The use of this handshape provides the signer with accuracy for describing things that are flat. Using the "flat" hand will empower you as a signer. As you acquire the following vocabulary for things around the house, you will see the power of the "flat" hand again and again.

◄ **HOME:** Tap and move the fingertips of the modified "O" hand from the corner of your mouth to the soft part of your cheek. *Variation:* The first variation is to tap the fingertips of the modified "O" hand twice on the soft part of your cheek. The second variation is to tap the fingertips of the flattened "O" hand near the corner of your mouth, then open to a "flat" palm against the cheek.

All of these signs represent "home" as the place where you would eat and sleep. Perhaps you are staying in a college dorm. There is an initialized sign for this word. To sign "dorm," tap and move the "D" hand from the corner of your mouth to the soft part of the cheek.

In Chapter 6, you learned how to sign "house" by making the shape of a roof with both "flat" hands. In Chapter 10, you learned how to make a "room," again using just both "flat" hands. Remember, to sign "room," use both "flat" hands and move them in a box shape to indicate two sets of walls; front and back, and both sides. This sign is also used for "box."

It is important to put to memory the sign for "room." This sign is used as an add-on when describing additional rooms around the house.

◀ **BEDROOM:** Place both hands, palm to palm, on the side of the face, imitating sleep, and add the sign for "room."

- To sign "living room," combine "live" (see Chapter 6) and "room"
- To sign "dining room," combine "food/eat" (see Chapter 14) and "room"

Each chapter introduces vocabulary and gives you an opportunity to build sentences and learn compound signs, as seen in these last two signs.

FACT

Alexander Graham Bell is best known for inventing the telephone. However, did you know that during his early career, he was a private tutor for the deaf? One of his most famous students was Helen Keller, whom he described as one of his most gifted students.

Take a quick look back at Chapter 10 and practice the following words.

- **"Floor":** Use the "flat" hands, palms down, thumbs touching, then separate them, imitating a flat surface.

- **"Wall":** Use the "flat" hands, palms out, thumbs touching, then separate them, imitating a wall.
- **"Window":** Use "flat" hands, palms facing your chest, right hand on top of your left hand, raise your right hand, imitating opening a window.

In Chapter 14, you learned how to sign "table." The next sign is a variation of "table," and one that will allow you to form different types and shapes of tables. To sign this next version of "table," use the "flat" hands, palms down, thumbs touching, then separate them, imitating a flat surface. To add legs to the table, use the "G" hands moving downward. You can mold and shape any type of table using these basic handshapes.

All of these signs use some form of the "flat" hand classifier. In this chapter, you begin to see the power and the multiple applications of classifiers, as described in Chapter 10.

The Telephone and the TTY

You use a variety of phones in communication, and so do the deaf. Today's technological advances in communication devices have made the world more accessible for the deaf and hard of hearing. Telephone services for the deaf used to be limiting. The TTY caller could only connect with other people with a TTY or use a relay service to provide assistance. There are now multifunctioning cell phones, along with a variety of other communication devices.

FACT

In 1964, Robert H. Weitbrecht, a deaf man, invented an electronic device called the acoustic coupler. The coupler enabled typewritten communication over the phone with the use of a teletypewriter.

There was a time when the TTY, a text telephone with a keyboard, a small screen, and an optional printer for the deaf, was uncommon and difficult to use. Today, TTYs are in use in places such as hospitals, police departments, fire departments, schools, and colleges. The American Disabilities

Act (ADA) mandates that public services providers must allow for equal access to communication for the deaf and hard of hearing.

If you work in any of the listed areas that are mandated to have TTYs, don't be afraid to use it. TTYs are user-friendly, just like text messaging.

Abbreviations Often Used

Many abbreviations often used during a TTY conversation are the same as those that are used in text messages. A few of the basic abbreviations are shown in this chart.

Relay Telephone Service

If a person does not own a TTY or have text messaging capabilities and needs to contact a deaf TTY user or vice versa, a telecommunications relay service (TRS) must be used. You can reach a relay telephone service assistant by dialing 711. This is how it all works:

Word	Abbreviation
Are	R
Because	CUZ
Go ahead	GA
Hold	HD
Oh, I see	OIC
Operator	OPR
Please	PLS
Question mark	Q
See you later	CUL
Should	SHD
Stop keying	SK
Thanks	THX
Tomorrow	TMW
You	U
Yours	UR

- Dial 711
- A relay communication assistant, or CA, answers.
- You tell the CA the TTY number you wish to call.
- The CA, using a TTY, dials that number.
- The CA will then become the voice of the deaf person by reading her typed text to you and speaking in the first person.
- Speak to the CA as if you are speaking directly to the person called. The CA will type everything you are saying to the deaf person.
- During a relay call, only one person can speak or type at a time.
- Both parties must say or type "Go Ahead" or "GA" to indicate it is the other person's turn to speak or type.

As you can see, this method is slow and sometimes awkward.

Technological Advances

Today, technological advances have certainly assisted in filling the communication gaps that the deaf have faced over many years. These new devices offer mobile services, text messaging, instant messaging, e-mails, paging systems, two-way real-time conversations on videophones, and now voice-to-caption telephones. The deaf and hard of hearing finally can stay connected any where, any time. In all probability, you already know and use the natural mime sign for "telephone" or "call." To sign "telephone," place the "Y" hand up to your ear, imitating talking on a telephone.

Computers

Computers have opened the door to the world. Web cameras on computers offer communication opportunities as never seen before for the deaf and hard of hearing. There are free services for the deaf and hard of hearing, enabling anyone to conduct video relay calls with family, friends, or businesses using certified ASL interpreters via a high-speed Internet connection and a video relay.

Computers are a way of life today, so learn some basic computer signs. Many of them are very easy and not as technical as you might think.

◄ **COMPUTER:** Place the "C" hand on the back of your left hand and move up the arm.

To sign "laptop/notebook": Place hands horizontally in front of you palm-to-palm. Next, fold back your right hand so the palm faces you, imitating opening a laptop. The bottom hand represents the keyboard portion, and the upper hand represents the screen, add the sign "computer."

◀ **FILE:** Place the "flat" hand, horizontal, palm up, between the index and the middle fingers on your left hand, then between the middle and the ring fingers. *Memory aid:* The open fingers of the left hand are the slots for the files.

◀ **PROGRAM:** Flip the "P" hand up over the tops of the fingers and down the back of the left vertical "flat" hand.

◄ **INTERNET/NETWORK:** Touch the fingertips of both middle fingers of your "open five" hands and pivot back and forth. *Memory aid:* This sign demonstrates connectivity with information moving back and forth.

In Chapter 6, you were shown the generic sign and initialized sign for "e-mail." Each variation has a different visual value and varying popularity.

▲ **E-MAIL 3:** To sign "e-mail," form the letter "C" with the left hand, pass the right flat hand through the "C" hand. This variation represents the iconic symbol shown on computers that depicts an envelope.

▲ **E-MAIL 4:** To sign "e-mail," form the letter "C" with the left hand, extend the right index finger, point forward, and pass through the letter "C." This sign can be reversed and represents contact in receiving mail.

◀ **DISK:** Circle the "D" hand in a double clockwise circle in your left upturned palm.

Here's another opportunity to combine two signs you have already learned: "computer" and "bug," (Chapter 13) equals a "virus." If you have a virus, you might need a firewall. This sign is a combination of "fire," shown here and "wall," shown earlier in the chapter.

◀ **FIRE:** Hold both "open five" hands, palms facing in. Wiggle your fingers while moving your hands alternately up and down.

To sign "cursor," move the "X" hand, palm forward, in an upward and forward jagged movement, and visualize the "cursor" moving all around the computer screen.

To sign "window" in relationship to computers, sign it the same way it was demonstrated earlier.

Abbreviations are used throughout the language of computers. Here's another chance to practice, improve, and build your fingerspelling skills.

Word	Abbreviation
Computer Disk	CD
Digital Video Disk	DVD
Central Processing Unit/Processor	CPU
Instant Messaging	IM
Software	SW
Gigabyte	GB
Megabyte	MB
Web	WEB
World Wide Web	WWW
Uniform Resource Locator	URL

This preceding group of signs has taught you something new and useful while providing you with the opportunity to review your fingerspelling skills. A good way to remember signs is to teach them to someone else. Perhaps you can share some of these signs with family or coworkers. Remember, to teach is to relearn.

School Days

Think back to your early years in elementary school. Visualize your teacher standing in front of the class, clapping her hands and saying, "Come on, children, it's time to settle down and put our thinking caps on!" Making visual associations, such as this one, adds clarity to the formation of some signs. Now get ready to play school and learn additional sign vocabulary.

To sign "school," clap your hands twice. You have made the sign for school, just like the teacher. In Chapter 9, you learned the sign for "teach."

The sign for "education" is formed in the same manner, this time using both "E" hands on the sides of your forehead and pushing forward slightly. This is another initialized sign.

There is a special way to demonstrate the school years, freshman through senior. Tap the right index finger on the appropriate finger of the left "open five" hand, like so:

- **Freshman:** tap the ring finger.
- **Sophomore:** tap the middle finger.
- **Junior:** tap the index finger.
- **Senior:** tap the thumb.

Another variation, using the same fingers, for indicating the school years: tap your right thumb, index, middle finger, or ring finger into the palm of the left hand.

School Subjects

Do you remember your favorite subject in school? Here are four subjects for you to sign.

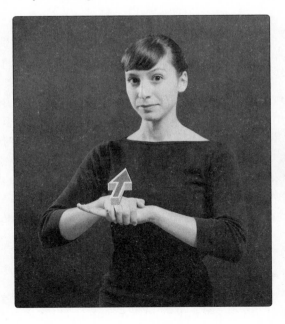

◀ **ENGLISH:** Use your right hand to cover the back of the left "flat" hand then pull it toward you.

▲ **MATH:** Cross the "M" hands repeatedly.

▲ **SCIENCE:** Use both alternating "A" hands, point thumbs down, and make a pouring motion, imitating measuring liquids from science beakers.

▲ **ART:** Use the "I" hand and draw a wavy motion down your left palm, imitating drawing.

Working in Education

This vocabulary is beneficial to all students of sign language, but it is most important for those who work in educational settings. Sit up straight, pay attention, and let's get down to business. In Chapter 6, the sign for "learn" was demonstrated: you place all the fingertips into your left palm, pull upward with a modified "O" hand, and place it on your forehead, imitating placing knowledge into your mind. If you are a student, you are in school to learn. In order to form the sign for "student," form the sign for "learn" and then add the "person" sign (Chapter 9). The sign for "book" is another natural gestural sign. Place both palms together then open, just like a book.

The next signs are all formed in the left palm just as you just signed "art."

- To sign "dictionary" use the "D" hand and stroke your left palm, imitating turning pages in a book.
- To sign "read," use the "V" hand, representing a pair of eyes, move left to right on your left palm, imitating reading.

- To sign "write," mimic writing on your left palm.
- To sign "graduate," form a clockwise circle with the "G" hand and bring it down into your left palm. Memory aid: The hand movement represents placing a seal on a diploma.

Punctuation

As you know, gesturing and mime are both part of ASL. With that in mind, let's learn how to form punctuation. All of the following punctuation marks are traced in the air exactly as though you were writing them. Remember to make these five punctuation marks large enough so that they can be seen easily by the sign reader.

Punctuation Mark	Symbol
Question mark	?
Exclamation point	!
Quotation marks	" "
Colon	:
Semicolon	;

The sign for "exam," "test," or "quiz" somewhat forms a double-handed question mark. Begin by using both index fingers of the "one" hands, while moving downward, change your index fingers into the shape of the letter "X," end with both hands in an "open five," palms down.

College Years

You are doing so well at this point that it's time to move on to the college level, to graduate, and to get your diploma.

◄ **COLLEGE, UNIVERSITY:**
Begin with your hands in the same position as "school." Swing your right hand in a counterclockwise upward arc.

Variations for college and university often use "initializations" while maintaining the same movement as just described. Here are a few examples:

- **College:** Use the right "C" hand
- **University:** Use the right "U" hand

◄ **DIPLOMA:** Touch the "O" hands together and draw them apart, imitating the shape of a rolled diploma.

As you progress through the material in these chapters, you are made aware of how important it is to know and have command of the handshapes of the alphabet. Another good way to practice fingerspelling is to use this table of abbreviations for specific academic degrees.

Degree	Fingerspelled Abbreviation
Bachelor of Arts	BA
Bachelor of Science	BS
Bachelor of Science in Nursing	BSN
Doctor of Dental Science	DDS
Doctor of Education	EdD
Education Specialist	EdS
Juris Doctor (law degree)	JD
Doctor of Medicine	MD

Working Nine to Five

Work is described in many different ways because it varies from one person to the other. Whether your job requires going to school full-time, taking care of children, or working as a service provider, it is all described as work. As shown in Chapter 6, to sign "work," use both "S" hands, palms facing down. Tap your right wrist on the back of your left fist a few times. The sign for work can have movement variations that are used to indicate intonation and degree of intensity. When signing "work," you can demonstrate how hard you might have worked by increasing the intensity and the speed with which one hand strikes against the other. Suppose you had a day at work when things went smoothly. You can also demonstrate this kind of easy workday by changing the intensity to a slower, softer tapping of the fists.

So it's off to work you go. The start and the end times of your job are very important. You've already learned some of the time signs in Chapter 12; therefore, you know how to point to your watch to indicate time. Now you'll learn how to sign "start" and "stop."

◄ **BEGIN, START:** Place the index finger of the "one" hand between the index and middle finger of your left hand and turn. *Memory aid:* Visualize placing the key in the ignition of a vehicle and turning it.

Don't limit the sign "start" just to the application of starting a vehicle. Think of this sign when you need to sign: "commence," "origin," "root," "initiate," "activate," "instigate," or "set in motion."

The sign for "start" can be combined with many signs you have already learned. With this exercise, your vocabulary expands from singles to pairs. Here's how it works. Start with a basic phrase describing a common action. You visualize this action then sign the words that make it into a series of complete sentences. As you sign the words in the sentences, don't hesitate to throw in a little mime and gesture. All the words in these three sentences you know how to sign. Visualization is a great tool. Use it, and you will sign successfully. (Reminder: you do not need to sign any of the little words people say daily, such as "the," "a," or "is.") Sign the following short sentences.

You wake up in the morning and then you . . .
- Start to make the coffee.
- Start cooking the breakfast.
- Start the car.

The simplest way to sign these sentences:
- Start coffee.
- Start cook breakfast.
- Start car.

Sign language is a visual language, and it is how you see the words not how you hear the words. This part of the journey often is the most difficult. Hang in there. Here are some more work related signs for you to learn:

◄ **STOP:** Use the side of your "flat" hand to hit your left "open" palm once.

▲ **FINISH:** Use "open five" hands, palms facing in, and snap them outward to the sides.

▲ **MAKE:** Place "S" hands one on top of the other, then twist them back and forth.

▲ **HELP:** Place the "A" hand in your left "open" palm and lift both hands upward.

In Chapter 4, you learned to sign the initialized version of "boss" by tapping the "B" hand on the heart. Another way to sign "boss" is to tap the "claw" hand on the right shoulder, representing the person who has the responsibility.

◄ **BEEPER/PAGER:** Hold the "S" hand at the waist, flick your thumb, index finger, and middle finger, imitating vibration or pulsing.

"Office" is an initialized sign and it is formed with the same movements as "room." To sign "office," use the "O" hands and move them in a box shape to indicate two sets of walls; front and back, and both sides

Presently, these signs for "fax" are the most popular versions:

- **"Fax":** Move the right "X" hand under the "flat" palm down left hand.
- **"Fax":** Form the letter "F" at the wrist of the left hand, then quickly change to "X" while sliding across the open palm to the end of the fingertips.

To sign "meeting," use "open five" hands held apart. Bring your hands toward each other while closing and touching the fingertips together.

In this chapter, you have been all around and about learning common everyday signs. Keep applying the signs you know, especially the signs you just learned, at home or at work daily.

CHAPTER 16

What's Up, Doc?

This chapter covers subjects in the medical arena, from signing "pain" to "doctor." You will be provided with information regarding the special considerations for the deaf and hard of hearing in a medical setting. This chapter also presents communication strategies, the inner workings of the ear, how to prevent hearing loss, as well as the latest information on cochlear implants.

In Sickness and in Health

There are over 28 million deaf and hard-of-hearing people in the United States. Many of them will need hospital, medical, or emergency care at some point in their lives. The anxiety associated with this experience is profound. A hearing person can only imagine the distress produced by the soundless images of the emergency room, operating room, recovery room, testing laboratories, medical equipment, and medical personnel in a hurry. Even more apprehension is generated for the deaf and hard of hearing by their fears of being isolated, misunderstood, and failing to understand questions and instructions.

Today, medical and hospital personnel all possess the ability to alleviate the kinds of problems encountered by the deaf and hard of hearing in medical situations and to deliver effective, quality care to them. Increased awareness, preventive actions, and simple considerations will ease many of the fears and apprehensions that accompany medical and emergency services.

FACT

Knowledge of ASL is the medical community's most effective line of communication. Establishing this mode of communication will help facilitate an accurate and quicker evaluation of a deaf or hard-of-hearing patient.

In addition to sign language, patients can, or may, use any one of these various methods of communication with medical staff:

- Lip reading
- Writing
- Gesturing and mime
- Use of hearing aids
- Speech
- Use of interpreters

Communication Strategies

The technological world of electronic medical records is quickly becoming the norm in doctors' offices, hospitals, and medical facilities. Deaf or hard-of-hearing patients are faced with medical personnel looking at computer screens and keyboards, with less face-to-face communication and limited eye contact. To improve interpersonal communication between medical personnel and deaf and hard-of-hearing patients, here is a list of very important communication strategies:

- Ensure that you are facing the deaf or hard-of-hearing patient.
- Maintain eye contact by looking directly at the patient's face.
- Do not turn away in the middle of a sentence.
- Speak clearly and in simple sentences, rephrasing rather than repeating.
- Speak naturally, not too fast, and do not shout.
- Do not exaggerate your lip movements.
- Allow more time for communication.
- Do not allow two people to speak at the same time.
- Face the light while speaking, eliminating shadows, and easing lip reading.
- Use pantomime, gestures, and facial expressions to assist you in communicating.
- Avoid technical terms and keep the information straightforward.
- Write important instructions in clear language.
- Provide an interpreter when the patient is unable to comprehend.
- Provide an interpreter when an injury or medical problem is complex.
- Speak to the patient, not to the interpreter.
- Explain medical procedures as they are being performed.

Specific Medical Considerations

Due to unintentional communication barriers, the deaf, and hard of hearing often need more support and explanation than is required for other patients.

If you are in the medical profession or are tending to a deaf person in any medical situation, keep the following suggestions in mind:

- When it is necessary for medical personnel to use masks, the use of clear masks should be used at all times when communicating with a patient who needs to lip read. Clear masks should be available at all medical facilities for personnel.
- Patients may need or want to use sign language; therefore, it is important not to restrict the patient's hands or arms. If possible, use the forearm area to insert any intravenous needle (IV). When placed in the back of the hand or the wrist area, IVs limit hand movement and cause discomfort. (This same rule applies to those patients who are not deaf or hard of hearing but who use sign language as a mode of communication with their family members.)
- Patients who are lying down will have difficulty lip reading. Try to speak from the same level. Only 30 percent of all language can be seen on the lips, even under the best of conditions. Do not assume you have been understood.
- The face of a patient should not be covered unless necessary. This is due to the importance of sight for comprehension. If vision is compromised for any reason, gentle and constant reassuring touching should be given.
- Always explain to a patient why you are leaving the room and when you are coming back. Do not just walk out. Patients should not be isolated or left in complete darkness.
- Do not engage in small talk. Although this is reassuring to hearing patients, it may cause deaf or hard-of-hearing patients to feel that they are missing important information, and they may become agitated and confused.
- Ensure that patients have access to their hearing aids, glasses, and a sign language interpreter when instructions are complicated. These are vital communication tools.

It is inappropriate both ethically and legally for medical personnel to use family members as interpreters. Specifically, it is extremely inappropriate to use children as interpreters in any medical situation.

◀ **SIGNER'S HANDS:** The "Signer's Hands" symbol denotes sign language interpretation is provided at the facility.

The "Broken Ear"

The "Broken Ear" is a national symbol that is used to publicly represent deafness and/or services for the deaf and hard of hearing. When this symbol is displayed within a hospital setting, it denotes the presence of a deaf or hard-of-hearing patient.

◀ **THE "BROKEN EAR"**

This symbol should be displayed or attached on the following:

- Admission form
- Patient identification bracelet
- Cover of the patient's chart   *(continued on following page)*

- All pertinent written and electronic medical records and information
- Intercom button at the nurse's station denoting the patient's room
- Head or foot of the patient's bed, with the patient's permission

Deaf and hard-of-hearing patients, when entering into medical situations, are always appreciative of medical personnel who can communicate in sign language. If you are considering a position in the medical field, it would be extremely advantageous to take a sign language course.

The medical world is working to bring about many changes and improvements for the health and care of our future populations. Nonetheless, the Rubella Bulge population will be getting older and will have their share of medical issues with increasing age. The medical community will find itself in need of more personnel with knowledge of sign language.

Hospitals and medical facilities eagerly hire staff who have knowledge or experience with sign language. Today, hospitals, physicians' offices, clinics, and all medical facilities must comply with ADA mandates, making sign language a sought-after skill.

First Aid

Warm up your hands and get ready to form a few signs that are appropriate to the medical setting. Your first medical lesson is an easy one. To sign the parts of the anatomy, all you need to do is simply point to the specific body part. Your second lesson will teach you how to form commonly used signs in the medical arena.

◄ **DOCTOR:** Place the "D" hand on the inside of your left wrist, imitating taking a pulse.

To sign "nurse," place the "N" hand on the inside of your left wrist, imitating taking a pulse.

To sign "medical," place the "M" hand on the inside of your left wrist, imitating taking a pulse. It would not be unusual to see a deaf or hard of hearing patient specifically sign "medical" in reference to a doctor or nurse.

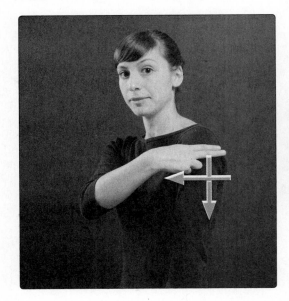

◄ **HOSPITAL:** Use the "H" hand to trace a cross on your left upper arm. *Variation:* Use the "H" hand to form the sign of a cross on the front of your chest in the area where a person would wear a name badge.

To sign "patient," use the "P" hand to trace a cross on your left upper arm.

▲ **SICK/ILL:** Use "open five" hands and touch the middle finger of your right hand to your forehead while simultaneously touching the middle finger of your left hand to your stomach. A facial expression of physical distress aids in emphasizing this sign.

▲ **EXAM:** Use both "C" hands moving alternately in a series of circles in front of your face, across your line of vision.

◄ **PAIN:** Point both index fingers toward each other and move them in a back and forth motion. *Variation:* To demonstrate severity of pain use the same handshape, adding a twist and turn motion. Both variations of this sign can be formed near or on the area of pain. Example, an "earache" would be signed with the index fingers pointing and jabbing toward the ear. A sore throat would be signed in the same manner, this time pointing to the throat, and so forth.

To sign "infection," slightly shake the "I" hand from right to left, palm facing forward.

To sign "blood pressure," first form the sign for "blood," then grasp your left upper arm, imitating the blood pressure cuff.

▲ **MEDICINE:** Move the middle fingertip of your right hand in small circles on the upturned palm of your left hand.

▲ **HEALTH/HEAL:** Place both "open five" hands on your chest then move away forcefully closing the hands into a tightly closed fist.

◀ **SURGERY:** Stroke the thumb tip of the "A" hand, palm facing down, across the chest or abdomen. *Variation:* Stroke the thumb tip of the "A" hand from the left hand fingertips across the palm to the wrist. The handshape and movement for "surgery" can also be formed and placed at the actual site of any incision or laceration.

◀ **BLOOD:** Place the right and left "open five" hands, palms facing your body. Move the right hand downward wiggling the fingers while brushing the back of the left hand.

▲ **BREATHE:** Move both "flat" hands to and from your chest, imitating the movement of breathing.

▲ **HEART:** Place both index fingers on the chest, trace the outline of the heart starting at the top.

To sign "heartbeat," first form the sign for "heart," then hit the back of your right "S" hand to your left palm at chest level a few times, imitating the heart beating.

To sign "heart attack," first form the sign for "heart," then hit the fist of your right "S" hand sharply to the palm of your left hand.

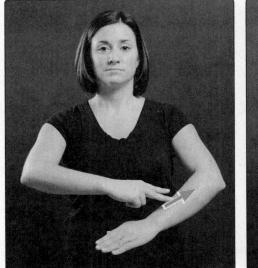

▲ **IV/INTRAVENOUS:** Slide the "V" hand into your forearm, imitating the placement of an intravenous line. *Variation:* Slide the "V" hand into the back of your hand.

▲ **OXYGEN:** Place the "curved" hand over your nose and mouth, imitating the shape of an oxygen mask. *Variation:* Place the index and middle fingers under each nostril, imitating nasal oxygen tubing.

In the medical arena, there are always questions to be asked. All you need to do is to form the shape of question marks. Don't forget to put the dots!

Exploring the Ear

The ear is a small and fascinating precision instrument. It receives sounds and transmits the information to your brain. But how does it really work? Here is a short voyage into the ear.

1. Sound waves carrying noise and speech are collected by the outer portion of the ear. These sound waves travel down the ear canal to the eardrum.

2. The sound waves cause the eardrum to vibrate. This in turn sets three ossicular bones—the anvil, the hammer, and the stirrup—in the middle ear into motion. The middle ear acts as a transformer, passing on the vibrations of sounds to the inner portion of the ear, known as the cochlea.
3. The vibration in the inner-ear fluid causes the hair cells that line the cochlea to move. The hair cells change this movement into electrical impulses.
4. These electrical impulses are sent up to the brain, via the auditory nerve, where they are interpreted as sound.

When damage occurs to the cochlea, the electrical impulses are not allowed to reach the nerve fibers that are responsible for carrying sound information to the brain.

Definition of Hearing Loss

A general description for deafness is the inability to hear and understand speech. Approximately one-fourth of the population represents this description. Here are two definitions of hearing losses:

-   A **conductive hearing loss** is damage that occurs to the outer or middle ear.
-   **Nerve deafness, or sensorineural hearing loss,** is damage that has occurred to the tiny hair cells within the cochlea. These damaged hair cells prevent the electrical impulses from reaching the auditory nerve fibers. Therefore, these fibers do not have information to send up to the brain.

The term "hard of hearing" is preferred over "hearing impaired" by the Deaf community and the hard of hearing when referring to individuals who have a hearing loss.

Caution: Fragile Ear!

Hearing loss is the number one disability in the world, and yet it is the most preventable disability in the world. It is important to realize the ear is made up of small and fragile parts. These fragile bones and hair cells have no defenses against loud noises that damage your hearing. In your everyday environment, you experience auditory nuisances that you cannot control; loud vehicles, traffic sounds, construction, dogs barking, crowd noises. However, there are self-induced damaging noises that you can control.

- Personal music devices constantly set on loud
- Car radios played loud enough to vibrate the car windows
- Exposure to extraordinarily loud music concerts or clubs
- Operating loud equipment without wearing ear protection

Unfortunately, musicians in rock bands playing loud music face a life of diminished hearing. The self-induced damage to your hearing is the reason why hearing loss continues to be the most "preventable" disability.

FACT

Each year, well-known musicians are honored by being inducted into the Rock and Roll Hall of Fame. The numbers among these inductees who have a hearing loss is greater than 60 percent.

To safeguard your hearing, always wear ear protection when operating any type of loud equipment. Importantly, remember to always use soft earplugs when attending rock concerts. You will still be able to hear the music without traumatizing your ears. Simply said: avoid loud noises, lower the volume, prevent damage, and save your hearing!

Signs of Hearing Loss

Approximately 28 million people in the United States are deaf or hard of hearing. Signs of a hearing loss in both adults and children include the behaviors listed on the following page.

- Saying "huh" or "what" frequently
- Requesting that things be repeated
- Turning the volume up on the television, radio, and personal listening devices
- Sitting close to the television with the volume turned up very loud
- Misunderstanding conversations
- Becoming confused with words that sound alike
- Inattentive at home, school, or social gatherings
- Withdrawn behaviors
- Turning of the head and leaning, favoring one ear or another
- Speaking loudly
- Staring at people who are speaking
- Answering questions incorrectly
- Inappropriate speech development

Decibel Ranges

Here is a simple overview of what people hear at various decibel ranges. A decibel, abbreviated as "dB," is a unit of measurement for the loudness of sound.

Decibel Range	Example of a Sound
0–10 dB	Birds tweeting, water dripping
10–20 dB	People whispering, ticking of a clock
20–40 dB	Quiet conversation
40–60 dB	Average conversation, baby crying
60–80 dB	Garbage disposal, dog barking, rush-hour traffic
80–90 dB	Motorcycle, lawnmower, leaf blower, subway train
90–100 dB	Truck, bus, power saw
100–110 dB	Emergency vehicle sirens, helicopter, outboard motor
110–120 dB	Rock bands, thunder
120 dB and above	Jet engine, fireworks, shotgun blast, dynamite

How does all this relate to your ability to hear the spoken word for the purpose of communication? The degree of loss certainly affects speech, the acquisition of language, and the ability to communicate readily. You will hear these descriptions when people are discussing hearing losses:

Decibel Range	Description
0–15 dB	Normal hearing
16–35 dB	Mild degree of loss. Likely to experience difficulty in communication; may miss 10 percent of speech.
36–50 dB	Moderate degree of loss. Likely to understand conversations within very close range, three to five feet. The probability of missing conversation beyond that range can be as high as 100 percent. Expressive speech may be affected.
51–70 dB	Moderate to severe degree of loss. Conversations must be extremely loud, and in all probability, 100 percent of speech is missed. Language acquisition is delayed, and speech intelligibility is reduced.
71–90 dB	Severe degree of loss. Delayed spontaneous language and speech. Likely to rely on visual communication.
91 dB plus	Profound degree of loss. Speech and oral language acquisition does not develop spontaneously. Speech is likely to be unintelligible. The person relies on vision for communication and learning.

Hearing Aids

The varying degrees of hearing loss provide a general description of what can occur to someone who hears at these levels. These descriptions do not take into account any of the benefits that come from assistive listening amplification systems (or hearing aids). Today there are multiple varieties of hearing aids available. This selection has greatly improved with the advances in hearing technology.

FACT

In the 1800s, different sizes and shapes of speaking tubes and ear trumpets were used to amplify sounds. They were held up to the ear and were extremely cumbersome. In the early 1900s, the batteries that powered hearing aids were so large that they were either carried in a box or strapped to the person's leg.

Our present-day technological advances allow hearing aids to make loud sounds softer and soft sounds louder. This improvement alone helps to eliminate the distortion factors that are created when sound is amplified. In addition, hearing aids come in a wide selection of sizes and styles, some of which can be worn in the ear canal or over the ear.

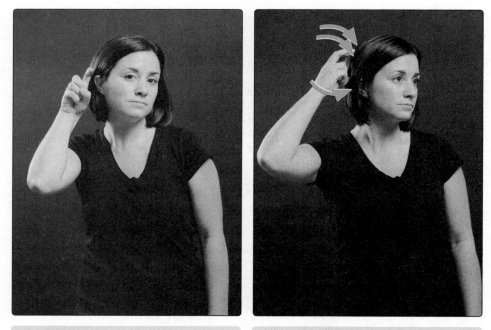

▲ **HEARING AID:** Hook the "X" hand over one or both ears.

▲ **COCHLEAR IMPLANT:** Tap the curved thumb, index finger, and middle finger behind your ear. *Variation:* Gently tap the "C" hand behind your ear.

Cochlear Implants

The cochlear implant (CI), invented in 1972, is an electronic device that provides a sense of sound to those who are profoundly deaf or severely hard of hearing. Since 1972, approximately 100,000 people worldwide have received cochlear implants. Often, a cochlear implant is referred to as a bionic ear. Perhaps it is best described as a prosthetic substitute for hearing.

How the Implant Works

A cochlear implant does not amplify sound, as hearing aids do, but instead stimulates functioning auditory nerves inside the cochlea with electrical impulses. Cochlear implants will not restore hearing or cure deafness. However, a cochlear implant can provide a useful representation of speech and sounds to appropriate recipients.

The newest CIs look like a large hearing aid. A CI has complex electronic components, internal and external. A surgical procedure is required for the implantation of the internal components. The external component is a speech processor that is a powerful minicomputer and is held in place behind the ear by a magnet component. The speech processor filters, analyzes, and digitizes sounds into coded signals that are sent to a transmitter and then on to a receiver/stimulator. The receiver/stimulator is the internal component of the CI. The cochlear implant takes over the function of the inner ear. Importantly, following the implantation of a CI, consistent and significant follow-up therapy is needed to acquire or reacquire a sense of hearing.

FACT

Heather Whitestone McCallum, Miss America of 1995, received a cochlear implant in August 2002. Since the implant, she has already heard a variety of sounds, such as water running from a faucet, a van door opening, and the sounds of her children. Heather continues to work on learning to interpret the more complex sounds she hears with her cochlear implant.

The entire time lapse between what the person hears and what the brain processes is microseconds. Presently, scientists are continuing to develop smaller, faster, enhanced speech processors. This will improve the perception of speech and music. During the upcoming years, one of the goals of the scientists is to also make these devices fully implantable.

The Cochlear Implant Education Center

Today, more than 100,000 adults and children worldwide have received cochlear implants according to the American Medical Association and the American Academy of Otolaryngology. The Cochlear Implant Education Center, on the campus of Gallaudet University, continues to investigate and evaluate cochlear implant technology and its role in the lives of deaf children, from birth to high school. The educational philosophy of the center for students with cochlear implants is to provide a linguistically rich environment for the acquisition of American Sign Language and English.

CHAPTER 17

Around the World

Everyone loves to plan that special get-away-from-it-all vacation. Traveling and seeing new places is always exciting. Whether you are planning a vacation, or whether you work in travel and tourism, this chapter offers interesting information, such as ADA mandates as they apply to hotels, regional variations in signs, travel directions, and related signs.

Sign Variations

Often, people wonder if signs are the same all across the United States. The answer is no. There are regional sign variations. These variations can be seen in the formation, placement, or direction of the signs. Nearly all large cities have variations in proper name signs. They also have fingerspelled abbreviations that are specific to the geographical area. For the most part, it is quite easy to adapt to these small and sometimes subtle sign differences. The variations can be compared to the various accents that you hear across the United States.

There are fun sign language books available that show you many of the sign variations. You will find some of them listed in Appendix B.

The variations in signs require signers to be flexible. Staying flexible is one of the important traits that will aid you in your journey to become a terrific signer. Keep in mind that the best signer is not necessarily the one who has the biggest sign vocabulary. The best signer is the one who knows how to *use* the vocabulary he has acquired.

While you are learning sign language, keep in mind the following list of positive traits that will help to make you a well-rounded signer. A good signer will do the following:

- Know more than one way to sign a word
- Be flexible in acquiring signed vocabulary
- Be flexible in applying a variety of signs
- Respect regional variations
- Inquire about variations in regional signs

On the Road Again

Have you ever wanted to be a world traveler? Now you can! Well, at least you can make a mental journey during this sign language lesson. You'll begin here in America and then travel to foreign countries.

◄ **AMERICA:** Interlock both "open five" hands and hold them in a nearly vertical position. Rotate hands counterclockwise. *Memory aid:* The fingers represent people joining and working in unison.

Canada is an easy sign to imitate. It represents shaking the snow off a coat. To sign "Canada," lightly tap the "A" hand on the upper part of your chest.

◄ **WORLD:** Rotate, the "W" hands away from you, around each other once. *Memory aid:* Demonstrates the revolving world.

◀ **COUNTRY:** Using the right "Y" hand, make a counterclockwise circle in front of your left arm close to your elbow. *Variation:* A "flat" hand can be used instead of a "Y" hand.

To sign "foreign" use the "F" hand.
To sign "Europe," circle the "E" hand near the right side of your forehead.

◀ **SPAIN:** Draw the "X" fingers from the shoulders and hook them together, in front of your chest. *Memory aid:* Imitates tying a matador's cape.

Often just a simple letter from the manual alphabet is used with a movement to sign a country. For example, to sign "France," hold the "F" hand palm in, then quickly turn your hand to palm-out position.

◄ **ITALY:** Use the "I" hand to draw a cross in the middle of the forehead.

◄ **GREECE:** Draw the "G" hand down your forehead and nose in a double movement. *Memory aid:* Imitates the profile of Grecian statues.

You have traveled over a small portion of Europe and must include England. Believe it or not, you already know how to sign this country. In Chapter 15, under "School Subjects," you learned how to sign "English." To form the sign for "England" and "Britain" you simply sign "English." Now let's take this sign a bit further, back to the United States, and learn how to form the sign for "New England."

New England is in the northeastern corner of the United States. To sign "New England" simply sign "new" and "England."

◄ **NEW:** Move the right "curved" hand, palm up, across the palm of your left hand from fingertips to heel, and off the hand in an upward arc.

Here are two interesting signs: the first imitates the shape of the country, and the second imitates the style of the country's traditional clothing.

◄ **JAPAN:** Touch the fingertips of both "G" hands together, then pull them apart to the side of your body, pressing your thumb tips and index tips together. *Memory aid:* Imitates the shape of the Japanese islands.

Abroad, one might see this sign being formed by imitating the sheath covering on a Samurai sword being pulled downward.

◀ **CHINA:** Point with your index finger to your left shoulder, cross to your right shoulder, and then draw the index finger straight down. *Memory aid:* This sign follows the lines of Chinese traditional clothing.

As a novice signer, be mindful when browsing ASL dictionaries—older signs can be disparaging. Cultural awareness and sensitivity is found in the newer versions of how signs are formed. Sign language has the capacity to communicate nonverbal respect and positive regard when describing other cultures.

FACT

A two-handed "manual alphabet" is used in Australian Sign Language (AUSLAN), British Sign Language (BSL) and New Zealand Sign Language (NZSL). In all three of these sign languages, only the letter "C" is formed with one hand.

Good examples are the signs previously shown for "America," which describes the melting pot of people coming together, "Spain," demonstrating the matador's cape, and "Greece" referring to its historical statues. These types of signs continue to demonstrate the beauty of sign language.

The Three-Finger Classifier

The "three-finger" classifier shows the movement or location of a mode of transportation. Normally, you would mime sign the words "car" or "drive" by imitating holding a steering wheel. You would use your hands to imitate a pedaling motion for the word "bicycle." Though both of these words have natural gestural signs, they cannot be used when trying to explain a car crash with the same freedom and exactness that the three-finger classifier provides.

▲ **TRAIN:** Rub the right "H" hand back and forth on top of your left "H" hand. *Memory aid:* Imitate railroad tracks.

▲ **AIRPLANE, JET, FLY:** Move your hand forward with your thumb, index finger, and pinky finger extended. Move with a bouncy movement for the noun, a steady movement for the verb.

◀ **BOAT:** Curve both hands together to form the bottom of a boat and move your hands forward in a wavy motion as if going through water.

Now that you know how to sign the modes of transportation, you can apply a three-finger classifier giving you freedom of movement.

◄ **THREE-FINGER CLASSIFIER:** The three-finger classifier is made with the thumb up and the index and middle finger extended.

Once you form this handshape, think of it as your mini-car. First, begin by forming the handshape with your left hand. Take a moment to closely look at the handshape. The index and middle fingers are the hood of your mini-car, the thumb is the seat, and the base of the thumb to your wrist is the trunk. You will need to imagine tires front and back on both sides of your little car. Now, use the thumb of your right hand to imitate a gas hose and place it at the rear of your car by the trunk. You can walk around, (use your inverted "V" right hand for legs) the car to check under the hood. To open the hood, lift your index finger. To sit in your car, drop your thumb inward to create a comfortable seat, then walk up, step into your car, and sit by dangling your fingers over your thumb. You can move your car sitting behind the imaginary wheel. This handshape easily demonstrates movement. For example, you can use this three-finger handshape to describe a car race and one car cutting off the other. Using both hands formed in the three-finger shape, line them up side by side, each hand representing a car and get ready, set, go.

Location and Direction

Signing directions is easy. Now that you know your ABCs, here is another chance to apply them. When giving directions to go north, south, east, or west, you will use initialized signs. Sign these four directions:

- North is indicated by moving the "N" hand straight up, skyward.
- South is indicated by moving the "S" hand straight downward.
- East is indicated by moving the "E" hand horizontally to the right.
- West is indicated by moving the "W" hand horizontally to the left.

While giving or receiving directions, it is always good to know when you are going up, down, right, or left. Sign the directions for these four signs:

- Right is indicated by moving the "R" hand horizontally to the right.
- Left is indicated by moving the "L" hand horizontally to the left.
- Up is indicated by the extended index finger pointing and moving upward.
- Down is indicated by the extended index finger pointing downward.

Time for a Vacation

Deaf people enjoy vacations the same as everyone else. However, they have justified concerns when staying at hotels. They need wake-up calls, visual smoke detectors, doorbells, and phones. Thanks to the ADA, the federal legislation that ensures hotels accommodate deaf and hard-of-hearing patrons, the stress related to vacations is seriously reduced. According to the ADA, the hotel shall provide the following accommodations for these patrons:

- Visual alarm clock
- Visual smoke alarm
- Telephone signalers
- TTYs
- Closed-caption decoders
- Doorbell notification

Thanks to these mandates, the deaf and hard of hearing no longer need to hand-carry their own visual signaling devices onto airplanes when they are traveling. Given the current status of baggage screening at airports, the ability of the deaf to travel lightly relieves a lot of stress and is very welcome.

Sign language on a resume is a wonderful enhancer. This is especially true when applying for a position as a service provider, in travel and tourism, as a park ranger, or any position that provides public services.

As discussed in Chapter 1, the need to provide services for the deaf and hard of hearing increases yearly. If your line of work is in hotel, travel, or tourism, your ability to use sign language will make everyone's travel experience pleasurable. To start you off in this area of signed vocabulary, here are five commonly used signs.

▲ **VACATION, HOLIDAY:** Place the thumbs of the "open five" hands at your armpits then wiggle your fingers.

▲ **TICKETS:** Grasp the left "flat" hand with the bent "V" hand, imitating punching a ticket.

◀ **VISIT, TRAVEL:** The "V" hands are rotated alternately, imitating people traveling. Rotating the "V" handshape away from you indicates that you are traveling. Rotating the "V" handshape toward you indicates people visiting you.

In the event that you are talking about animal travel, all you need to do is make a small change; form a bent "V" and move forward in a zigzag fashion. With one hand, you could demonstrate a bunny hopping; with both hands, you could demonstrate a leopard stalking.

Vacation always means packing, whether it's the car or the luggage. You know how to sign "vacation," now you need to know how to sign "luggage." The magic word is mime-sign. To sign "luggage," imitate lifting the handle of the luggage. However, with the new style of "luggage," you would imitate pulling a piece of luggage that has wheels.

◀ **ROAD:** Place both "flat" hands palms facing, move both hands forward.

Many different variations can be applied in the sign for "road." If the road is narrow or wide, bring your hands closer or farther apart. When the road or path is a winding way, simply demonstrate this by moving your hands in a wavy fashion. By using your "R" or "W" hands in the same fashion, the sign for road can be initialized. Knowing this little piece of information might save someone from becoming lost trying to find a street, way, avenue, or road. You have the ability to demonstrate the difference along with the new-found ability to give directions.

Here is a fun sign that closes your journey around the world.

◀ **HELICOPTER:** Form the three-finger classifier. Place an "open five" hand on the tip of your thumb and shake your right hand demonstrating the movement of the blades of the helicopter.

Bon Voyage!

CHAPTER 18

New Age of Sign Language

Using sign language with babies is a great way to get your baby started into language acquisition. Today, research is proving that teaching simple baby signs to your infant, toddler, or preschooler assists his or her development and raises IQ scores. In this chapter, you will learn the recommended first signs for babies. There is also information for early child care educators and sign language in classrooms as well as a healthy hearing baby checklist.

18

Baby Talk

Babies understand signs and are able to sign before they know how to talk. The reason for this is simple. Babies are able to manipulate their little hands long before they can manipulate their mouths to articulate words. Babies understand natural gestural signs. Surely you've seen a baby respond to the gestural language of a pair of outstretched arms and the facial expression of a big smile.

Benefits of Sign Communication

Early sign communication with babies produces significant benefits, including the following:

- Reduces frustration
- Improves communication
- Stimulates language acquisition
- Enhances intellectual development
- Improves confidence and self-esteem
- Increases memory, fine motor coordination, and attention skills

Recommended Baby Signs

Signing with baby is fun and enjoyable. It also will strengthen the parent-to-infant bond. Begin signing from the age of four to six months, when baby's focusing skills develop. Start out simply with just one or two signs, such as "milk" and "mommy." Reinforce these signs by signing them repeatedly. This repetition allows the baby to start to make the connection between the signs and the objects. Continue to build vocabulary with your baby daily. At eight to nine months of age, expect to see your baby start to sign back. Of course, the timing is variable; infants develop at their own rate. It is important to remember that signing with your baby encourages speech development. Babies who sign have approximately fifty more words at twenty-four months than nonsigning babies.

Recommended signs for infants:

Mommy	Chapter 5
Daddy	Chapter 5
Milk	Chapter 14
Eat	Chapter 14
Cookie	Chapter 14
Cat	Chapter 13
Animal	Chapter 13

If you are a parent of a young infant, it is exciting to know that you have already learned seven of the recommended signs. Along with those, you already know how to sign "baby"; it is signed by cradling a baby in your arms, and then rocking.

▲ **WANT:** Pull both "curved five" hands toward your body.

▲ **MORE:** Tap the fingers of both flattened "O" hands together.

Signing with your baby also has great benefits during the formative first two years of life. The "terrible twos" will be less frustrating for you and baby because of your nonverbal communication. In addition, it is wonderful to realize that by signing with your baby, you have enhanced cognitive skills, language, and speech formation. So just keep signing consistently with your baby. Keep a journal of your baby's sign language progress, and include many photos of baby signing. Someday, that journal will become a very special keepsake.

FACT

In newborns, the incidence of severe to profound hearing loss occurs in anywhere from five to thirty babies out of every 10,000 born. Later in this chapter, you will be provided with a list of signs that indicate healthy hearing in your child.

Toddler Classroom

You have introduced baby signs into your child's world during the first two formative years and have been pleased with the results. Now you are faced with selecting an early education child care center. You have worked diligently with your child to enhance all the parameters of learning. As a parent, you desire to have the learning enrichment continue in your choice of an early education center. Choose a center that applies sign language into the daily learning activities of your child. Do not be afraid to inquire if the staff use signs and if sign language is part of their learning and play curriculum. Ask to see the center's sign language materials or ask the staff to describe to you a daily signing activity. An early education center that uses sign language in your child's daily learning activities is a center that also recognizes the benefits.

Sign Language and Early Education

Sign language in the classroom provides an opportunity for early education providers to expand their preschool approach in teaching language arts, mathematics, science, social science, health, and the arts. Signing is a rich and exciting learning experience that appeals to all the senses—visual, spatial, verbal, physical, tactile, artistic, and musical. In addition, sign language assists in breaking down language barriers and opening pathways for communicating with special-needs children.

Today, early education specialists and child care providers are attending sign language classes and in-service training. Early education providers who have taken sign language are eager to incorporate signs into daily lesson plans. These educators know that sign language can keep children focused, increase memory, enhance language, and build their cognitive skills. They also have learned that they can manage children's behavior with nonverbal commands. If you are an educator or child care provider who has considered incorporating sign language into your classroom, you already have a head start with this book in hand. In fact, you can easily begin right now by applying signs in your daily classroom curriculum activities. Here's a quick review of some of the skills you have learned in the previous chapters:

- Manual alphabet
- Asking and answering questions
- Describing people
- Clothing and articles
- Colors
- Numbers

- Animals
- Foods
- Days of the week
- Emotions
- Verbs

These sign groups can be implemented into daily games in the classroom. You can begin with a letter of the manual alphabet and make it the letter of the week (see Chapter 4). Colors are easy to teach and can be applied in an array of games, including rainbow songs (see Chapter 7). Days of the week can be signed in games and songs (see Chapter 13). Weather signs can be applied to "What is the weather today?" The addition of animal signs to games, stories, or songs adds visual excitement for children. The next time you read *Brown Bear*, sign the colors and animals and watch the children's eyes shine with delight (see Chapters 7 and 13). The application of the signed images in this book is an endless resource for your classroom curriculum.

SIGNS FOR COMMUNICATING WITH BABIES

▲ **PLAY:** Pivot both "Y" hands several times.

▲ **GAME:** Use both "A" hands and tap knuckles together.

▲ **BAD:** Place the "flat" hand palm down on your chin, and toss your hand downward.

▲ **GOOD:** Place the "flat" hand to your chin, then bring the hand down palm-up and place it into your left open hand.

▲ **DIRTY:** Wiggle four fingers, palm down, under your chin. Don't forget to make a scrunched-up face. Facial expression is extremely important!

Hearing Health

For parents it is advisable to ensure that your baby has normal hearing and that your little one continues to stay healthy. To help you with this, here is a hearing health checklist for babies according to age.

Birth to Three Months
- ❑ Responds to sounds with blinks, or may be startled
- ❑ Attentive when hearing an unfamiliar noise or being called
- ❑ Awakens at loud sounds
- ❑ Responds to parents' voices
- ❑ Creates cooing noises
- ❑ Responds to noisy stimuli in the environment

Four to Five Months
- ❑ Responds to sounds by turning the head and eyes

Six to Nine Months
- ❑ Responds to nearly all environmental sounds
- ❑ Looks in the appropriate direction of sounds

Nine to Twelve Months
- ❑ Begins to imitate simple words
- ❑ Begins to use voice to get attention

Be cautious with your baby's hearing by always maintaining hearing health safeguards. The purpose of these safeguards is to keep loud damaging noises from entering into your baby's surroundings and into those fragile little ears. Your baby's ears cannot tolerate the loud volume that adult ears can. Noises that can be damaging and often not given enough consideration include the following:

- Vacuum cleaners today are powerful and loud. Avoid or limit exposure of your baby to this type of damaging sound.
- Excessively loud TV and music played in the house. Turn down the volume for your baby's hearing health.

- Excessively loud music played in the car. Your baby is strapped into the car seat in the back of the car, the same area where the large speakers are installed. The moment the music is turned up to an excessive volume, your baby's hearing is instantly at risk.
- Loud events such as concerts, fireworks displays, and auto races are damaging to ears. Your baby or young child will need you to provide her with good ear protection.

Hearing health safeguards should be part of the daily routine. Hearing loss is the number one most preventable disability, and it begins with you, the parent.

Simplified Signs

Simplified signs are signs that have been modified and are used in an adaptive manner for special populations. These populations might include special-needs students or those with physical challenges and language limitations. The tendency when modifying signs is to simplify the formation of the sign itself. This simplification creates an ease of movement for those with limitations. In addition, these signs are often more iconic, made to closely resemble the word that is being signed.

E-QUESTION

What is an iconic sign?
An iconic sign is a pictorial representation. The formation, shape, and/or movement of an iconic sign can closely represent the visual imagery of the word.

Various programs have adopted the use of adaptive signs successfully. Keep in mind that these modified, simplified signs are not part of pure ASL. However, signs that have been adapted to serve specific populations truly have a positive impact and effect. Often, when these particular populations are given sign language as a means of enhancing communication, the modified, simplified signs decrease the frustration felt by these individuals. Generally, the signs are single vocabulary words and are used and applied in a manner similar to the home signs discussed in Chapter 1.

Many Faces of Sign

As you've learned, there are many wonderful applications for sign language, and these applications extend beyond the Deaf community. An interest in this mode of communication is on the rise. However, this interest creates some concern within the Deaf community for their beloved language. Some contend that changes, modifications, simplifications, and misuse all have the potential to corrupt the pure ASL. However, all languages evolve and change over time. A language has to be flexible enough to bring in the new and do away with the old.

During an average year, any Deaf community member, native signer, or interpreter might come up with a new sign purely out of necessity. A good example of a new sign is the one that applies to the ever-changing world of technology, "e-mail." Of course, there will be regional variations on new signs. Newly created signs that prove to be useful, easy to form, and are quickly recognizable will be the signs that are accepted by the Deaf community. As the saying goes: "Necessity is the mother of invention."

CHAPTER 19

Expressing Yourself with Signing

Learning to sign a song can be one of the most satisfying challenges for the novice signer. You'll also find that dancing and signing can be combined to create an exciting visual. Combining sign language with all its facial expressions and body language adds emphasis to a stage performance and easily translates to an audience. Get ready to take a bow.

Signing Music

Signed music is visually enchanting. It is also a great way to practice sign language. Adults quickly learn to enjoy signing music, and it is good exercise too. Children learn to love it because it's fun, and at the same time, it improves motor skills. In addition, signing the words to a song enhances memory skills for young and old alike. Once a child or adult signs a song, she easily remembers the lyrics and rarely forgets them.

FACT

On May 7, 1824, Ludwig van Beethoven's Ninth Symphony was performed in Vienna. Beethoven by this time was completely deaf and could not conduct the premiere. He did, however, stand next to the conductor. At the end of the performance, he remained unaware of the applause of the emotional audience until a soloist had him turn to face them.

When you approach the idea of signing music, it is best to do first things first. The first thing you need to do is select an appropriate song for your maiden voyage. You will play and sign your song many, many times before you satisfactorily sign it, so consider choosing a song that you enjoy hearing each time it plays. It is best if you select one for which you already know the lyrics. You don't want to learn how to form new signs and try to memorize new lyrics at the same time. The lyrics should be simple with clear meanings. Conceptual songs are difficult to translate from English to sign language, and for the novice signer, this will pose an additional problem. Therefore, it is a good idea to keep it simple.

Your song should not be excessively slow or fast, as these types of tempos require a high level of control while moving the signs to the music. Also, try to select a song that has repeating lyrics. The repetition will assist you in controlling the signs and, at the same time, build your rhythm. To wrap it all up for you in one statement: select a song you enjoy, one with simple lyrics you know, and one that has a moderate tempo. Place these considerations at the top of your list, and you will be well on your way to signing a good song.

Translating to Signs

Once you've chosen a song, you'll then need to look at the lyrics carefully and begin the process of translating them from English to signs.

- Write down all the lyrics, line by line.
- Omit all the small words, such as "a," "the," "is," and "of."
- Write the approximate sign equivalents of the words or concepts of the lyrics.

Go with the Flow

The translation of a song may require a few attempts before it is just right. Once you have mastered the appropriate signs, you can begin to connect them with the rhythm of the song. The time you put into this mode of signing will really show. Here are six helpful tips:

1. When translating the lyrics from English to signs, always think of what the lyrics are really trying to convey.
2. When practicing, sign your song three times in a row, take a break, and start over again.
3. Feet should be slightly apart, never together, thereby giving you the ability to flex and flow with the music.
4. Always use appropriate facial expressions and body language that matches the lyrics.
5. Never drop your hands to your sides while signing your song. Doing so stops the music visually.
6. Sign your song with the music, never without.

FACT

Phyllis Frelich won the Tony Award for Best Actress in the Broadway play *Children of a Lesser God*. Miss Frelich is profoundly deaf. In 1991, she also became the first deaf person to be elected to the Screen Actors Guild Board in Hollywood.

Don't be discouraged if you cannot fully sign your song in the first few attempts. Practice your song repeatedly and you will get there. The time you put into it will give you the desired results. Try to make the learning process and the practice all part of the fun of signing a song.

Practicing and learning new signs for music builds confidence in your new signing abilities. The simplicity of learning to sign a song will also stimulate you, perhaps without realizing it, into applying many of the basic principles of ASL. These principles range from translating English to signs, applying facial expressions, and using body language.

◄ **MUSIC, SONG:** To sign "music" or "song," sweep your right "flat" hand from the fingertips of your left open palm all the way up your arm and back down. This sweeping movement can be made several times and it can also be formed in a figure eight.

Heart and Soul

Religious hymns and songs expressed with the added element of sign language are powerful. They seem to help lift one's faith. The signs for heaven, soul, and angel are remarkably beautiful.

◄ **HEAVEN:** Use "flat" hands, palms facing each other, Cross your hands and arms above your head in an arched movement and spread your arms open.

◄ **ANGEL:** Place fingertips of both "bent" hands on your shoulders, then twist forward and out off your shoulders, imitating wings.

Visual Tapestries Within the Arts

Blending sign language and music often touches and emotionally moves audiences with its beauty. Combining dance with sign language also creates a visual delight. It adds a wonderful extension to a dance performance. The same is true of a stage performance that has been extended with manual signs and strong facial expressions. A signed song can be likened to creating an enchanting visual tapestry, a tapestry on which graceful signs with pleasant facials and body language are all woven together, to bring music to visual life. These visual tapestries within the arts are delightful, enjoyable, and appreciated by young and old, signing and nonsigning alike.

Developing Expressions and Body Language

Try this visualization exercise to work toward developing facial expressions and body language. The following signs have been previously shown to you in earlier chapters. Now you're going to sign while adding the elements of facial and body language. This time, there are no photo illustrations to guide you. Instead, you will find only the word, followed by the appropriate facial expression and body language.

As you know, facial expressions and body language are very important parts of sign language. Remember, they add an element of clarity and comprehension. The chart on the facing page will assist you in developing and enhancing these important elements. You will need to take a moment to look at the word and visualize what you see.

Building all the required elements into your signing requires some talent in the area of multitasking. Don't become frustrated at the beginning if you can't do it all. Instead, slowly learn to take on the character and posture of what it is you are trying to express or convey. Simply explained, you need to have a smile when you sign "happy," not wear a frown. The same is true in reverse. If you are signing "angry," show the appropriate facial. Start slowly, and practice the facial and body language described in the chart.

Continue practicing until you become comfortable with these postures. Before you even realize it, adding the appropriate facial expressions and body language will become second nature.

Sign/Word	Facial Expression	Body Language
Crazy	Rolling eyes, tongue out	Side-to-side head movement
Dictionary	Eyes down, looking studious	Turn slightly left from the waist up
Flower	Bright-eyed and pleased	Smell the fragrance, head tilts, shoulders up
Happy	Large, bright-eyed smile	Loose and relaxed neck and head
Lion	Fierce look, furrowed brows, focused eyes	Proud, powerful posture
Mirror	Admiring look	Head tilts side to side, chin up slightly
Motorcycle	Determined	Body forward, head down slightly, hands gripped
Napkin	Proper look, lips tightly together	Chin up, head tilted back slightly
Proud	Smiling, smug look, lips together	Shoulders back, chest out, chin up
Strawberry	Lips pursed as in kissing	Chin up, right shoulder rolls

The Art of Drama

Drama is a living art form and it is enhanced when combined with the visual form of sign language. Your signing skills become a valuable tool when applied in role playing, a theater group, a drama workshop, or in an educational setting. The addition of a few signs can add emphasis to lines in a play while reaching out to the audience in the back row. When singing a love song, sign the word "love"; it is a great way to show expression. Sign language has the unique ability to add depth to a character and provide an amazing visual impact. Whether you are singing a song, playing a role on stage, or acting out a story in a classroom, enhance all of these situations with the signs you have learned. Explore and demonstrate your own artistic creativity. Use the signs you have learned and remember to add facial expressions and body language. Geared up with all of the skills that have been introduced to in this and previous chapters, go ahead, express yourself, have fun, and show the beauty of sign language combined with your own talents and expertise.

CHAPTER 20

Further Your Skills

In this chapter, you'll find a variety of topics and skills to further your sign language education. First you'll learn a few more common signs that you'll need to use in everyday conversations. Then you'll take a look at a couple of new methods of communication just to give you an idea of what's out there in the signing community. You're also going to find out just how much you've learned and discover a few fun games to reinforce your signing skills.

Everyday Chatter

Common expressions used in everyday chatter follow. Some of these you've already learned, but it's always good to refresh your memory. You'll be able to use these words several times a day, so take advantage of each and every chance you have to practice your new skills on others.

ALERT!

A sign does not exist for every word. Classifiers can represent these words through shape and placement in a creative and clear manner. Another option would be to point to the item, when possible.

In Chapter 1, "hello" was the very first sign that this book introduced to you. Now here you are in the last chapter, look how far you've come.

The signs for "hello" and "goodbye" are natural, gestural signs. People pass this exchange every day by simply waving the "flat" hand.

Here are some other everyday signs:

▲ **PLEASE:** Circle the "flat" hand on your chest.

▲ **THANK YOU:** Place the fingertips of the "open" palms on your chin, then bring them down, palms facing up. This sign demonstrates a very courteous "thank you."

As shown in Chapter 6, to sign "yes," shake the "S" hand up and down while nodding your head up and down in affirmation. To sign "no," bring the extended thumb together with the index, and middle fingers. Remember to make a head negation when forming the sign for "no."

◄ **KNOW, KNOWLEDGE:** Place the "flat" hand at your temple.

To sign "don't know," form the sign for "know," then toss the hand off the temple.

Using Games to Learn

Games are a great way to practice fingerspelling and signed vocabulary while having fun and learning. The games presented here are simple sign language games for beginners, with easy-to-follow instructions. Teachers, early childhood educators, parents, adults, and children alike can all share in the fun.

The first game is the chain name game. The first player fingerspells his name. The second player fingerspells the first player's name and adds his own. The game continues around the room until it comes back to the first person, who spells the entire group's names.

The next game asks you to fingerspell by touch. One player fingerspells, while the other player, with eyes closed, tries to read the word by the feel of the handshape against his hand. Fingerspelling by touch is challenging, yet at the same time it is very interesting. In order to enjoy this game at its fullest, begin by fingerspelling three-letter words. When you have mastered the list of three-letter words, move on to words of four letters, then five, and so on.

Here is another fun game: One player signs food and cooking items, while the other players write the signed words out. It is easier to form the signs than it is to read the signs. This game will provide you with a way to have fun and practice at the same time.

This next game puts your number acquisition to the test. Exchange the following information using fingerspelling and numbers: age, shoe size, license plate number, cell phone, work, and home phone numbers, family members' ages, and zip code.

This game presents you with a challenge of applying facial and body language. One player acts out a function of a household object, and the other players guess the item. Examples: cutting meat equals "knife"; washing hands equals "soap"; unlocking door equals "key"; and sleeping equals "bed."

For the next game, one player fingerspells a clue, and the other players must guess the sport. Examples: "tee" equals "golf" and "bow" equals "archery." Apply variations by changing the groups to household items, office supplies, or things that are associated with recreation, places, and movies.

Charades

Charades is a word guessing game. A player uses physical activity instead of verbal language to convey a word. Now that you have acquired the skill of several everyday signs, you will have a major advantage. Throughout this book, you have used physical activity to convey language. Many signs you have learned are also "standard signals" in charades, such as "question," "past tense," and "book." So go ahead, initiate a game of charades with your family and friends. This game is a great way to practice signing and be a terrific champion while playing.

Magic Wand Game

This game facilitates and increases the use of facial expressions, body language, and pantomime. As you develop your signing skills, this list will be useful to you. Until then, you will be able to simply use them just like a game of charades. Use an imaginary wand whose dimensions are described with the use of classifiers and mime. Players may sign additional information to give more clues while describing the item. Sign these items using the imaginary wand and facial expressions, body language, or pantomime.

conductor's baton	baseball bat	hammer
screwdriver	thermometer	rolling pin
pencil	cane	paintbrush
ruler	straw	pogo stick
golf club	umbrella	mop/broom
cigarette	toilet brush	flagpole
drumstick	lipstick	toothpick
violin bow	nail file	stick of gum
spoon	sewing needle	crowbar
telescope	meat thermometer	jackhammer
pipe	toilet tissue holder	garden hose
knitting needle	belt	letter opener
crochet hook	window shade	curling wand
flute	bicycle pump	oil/transmission stick
bubble wand	toothbrush	bathroom towel bar
fishing pole	curtain rod	empty paper towel tube
plunger	can of room spray	yoke for carrying buckets
mascara	turkey baster	weed trimmer
computer mouse	tennis racket	telephone pole
washing machine	umbrella	cookie tin
remote control	candle	ironing board

Now that you have tried gesturing and miming the magic wand items, you need to try practicing a few of them applying classifiers. The next time you use this chart, visualize each item, then shape each item using the classifiers. The classifiers make it easier to describe things that are cylindrical, flat, thin, or vertical, as discussed in Chapter 10.

Total Communication

Total Communication (or TC) emphasizes the use of all methods of communicating. The benefit of TC is that it opens all the doors, using every practical mode to teach vocabulary and language. The final goal is to communicate using any and all methods with the deaf and hard of hearing and perhaps the special-needs child.

The following is a list of some of the methods used in TC:

- American Sign Language
- Signed Exact English
- Contact Sign Language/Pidgin Sign English
- Fingerspelling
- Lip reading
- Body language
- Facial expressions
- Oral speech
- Simultaneous communication, or sim-com (speech and signs used at the same time)
- Auditory/Verbal
- Cued speech (see following page)
- Amplification devices
- Writing
- Drawing
- Pantomime

Cued Speech

In 1966, Doctor R. Orin Cornett at Gallaudet University developed cued speech. This visual communication system has been adapted for more than fifty languages. Cued speech is a method whereby the speaker adds eight handshapes in four different locations to distinguish between similar sounds. This adds clarity to the spoken language by identifying each distinctive speech sound. It is used for phonic instruction; articulation therapy; and for individuals, regardless of the etiology, who have difficulty with speech. Some late-deafened adults rely on the assistance of cued speech for lip reading and maintaining their functional speech control.

A Quick Pop Quiz

You are drawing very close to the end of your lessons, and it's time for a pop quiz to see how much you remember. (No peeking at the answers!)

1. What is an iconic sign?_____

2. How do you become skilled in sign language? _____

3. Is sign language the same everywhere?_____

4. How do you ask questions? _____

5. How are differences in gender indicated? _____

6. What is the signing space? _____

7. What is a sign? _____

8. How do I make a sign for someone's name? _____

9. How do you indicate past, present, and future?_____

10. What is the Deaf community?_____

How do you think you did? Turn the page for the answers.

1. An iconic sign is a pictorial representation and can closely resemble the visual image of the word.
2. You become skilled in sign language with practice, practice, and practice.
3. Sign language differs from region to region and around the world.
4. You ask questions by leaning forward with a quizzical facial expression and eyebrows down.
5. Gender is indicated by the placement and location of the sign: forehead for male, jaw line for female.
6. Signing space is where most of the signs are formed. It encompasses the area from the top of the head to the waist.
7. A sign is a unit of language that is formed with distinctive handshapes, locations, specific movements, facial expressions, and body language.
8. People's names may be fingerspelled, or they may have a unique name sign.
9. Past is indicated by a backward movement. Present is formed directly in front of the body. Future is a forward movement from the body.
10. The Deaf community is a cultural group of people who share common values, language, and experiences.

Variety of Communication

Now that you have achieved a fundamental understanding of sign language, perhaps you will continue your learning and join the many faces of sign. Maybe you will be the new face in an ASL classroom or Deaf community. Signers are all around you. They are educators, medical personnel, and a broad spectrum of service providers, and their numbers are growing. There is no limit to the uses of sign language, and the variety of communication applications. Your education does not have to end when you close this book. Your personal motivation will guide you to find opportunities to practice and use signs. Search local communities for resources that can help you reach a greater proficiency in American Sign Language and build your confidence.

Your journey has just begun into this visual, interesting, and fun-filled language. Best of luck in your continued journey!

Quizzes and Games

Alphabet Quiz

Fill in the blanks with the appropriate letter from the manual alphabet.

1. To form the letter _____, cross the index and middle fingers. Thumb, ring, and pinky fingers are tucked into the palm.

2. To form the letter _____, all fingers are vertical with the thumb to the palm.

3. To form the letter _____, make a fist, hold the pinky finger vertical.

4. To form the letter _____, place the thumb between the index and middle fingers. Ring and pinky fingers are tucked into the palm. Drop your wrist downward.

5. To form the letter _____, make a fist. Tuck the thumb between the index and middle fingers.

6. To form the letter _____, extend the thumb and pinky finger. Tuck index, middle, and ring fingers into the palm.

7. To form the letter _____, curl all fingers down on the thumb except for the index finger, which remains vertical.

8. To form the letter _____, place the thumb between the index and middle fingers, held vertically. Ring and pinky fingers are tucked into the palm.

9. To form the letter _____, pinch the index finger to the thumb. Middle, ring, and pinky fingers are vertical.

10. To form the letter _____, place your index finger on top of your middle finger facing left, with the thumb tucked away behind the two fingers.

True/False Awareness Quiz

Read each question and circle the appropriate answer.

True or False   **1.** The first school for the deaf was established in 1817 in Hartford, Connecticut.

True or False   **2.** The uppercase word "Deaf" refers to the Deaf community, which shares a common language, cultural heritage, and similar interest.

True or False   **3.** American Sign Language, known as ASL, is the natural native language of the American Deaf Community.

True or False   **4.** Genders are indicated by forming male signs near the forehead and female signs on the chin or jaw line.

True or False   **5.** The Deaf community is a group of deaf people who share common values, language, and experiences.

True or False   **6.** Maintaining eye contact at all times with the signer is extremely important.

True or False   **7.** The structure of the signs is formed the same way whether you are right or left-handed.

True or False   **8.** A gesture is an expressive body movement that can convey an idea, feeling, or concept.

True or False   **9.** An interpreter is a person who facilitates communication between the deaf, hard of hearing, and hearing persons by translating spoken language into sign and vice versa.

True or False   **10.** The manual alphabet represents the thirty-six letters of the English alphabet.

Letter Form Quiz

Read each question and circle the appropriate answer.

1. Circle the seven letters of the alphabet that are formed with a closed hand.

   A B C D E F G H I J K L M N O P Q R S T U V W X Y Z

2. Circle the thirteen letters of the alphabet that are formed in a vertical position.

   A B C D E F G H I J K L M N O P Q R S T U V W X Y Z

3. Circle the two letters of the alphabet that are formed in a horizontal position.

   A B C D E F G H I J K L M N O P Q R S T U V W X Y Z

4. Circle the two letters of the alphabet that are formed pointing downward.

   A B C D E F G H I J K L M N O P Q R S T U V W X Y Z

Sign Practice Quiz

Read each question and fill in the blank with the appropriate word.

1. To sign "_____" place your palm on your chest.

2. To sign "_____" cross and tap the "H" hands twice.

3. To sign "_____" clap hands twice.

4. To sign "_____" stroke the "curved" hand twice on the left "flat" palm.

5. To sign "_____" raise both hands high in the air in an "open five" position and shake them.

6. To sign "_____" draw the "T" hand down the cheek.

7. To sign "_____" squeeze one or both "S" hands alternately up and down.

8. To sign "_____" place the fingertips of the "open" palms on the chin, then bring down the palms facing up.

9. To sign "_____" place all the fingertips into the left palm. Next, pull upward with a modified "O" hand and place it on the forehead.

10. To sign "_____" place the "flat" hand to the chin, then bring the hand down, palm up, and place it in the left palm.

11. To sign "_____" use the "flat" hand, move it forward and down.

12. To sign "_____" place both "flat" hands palms facing, move both hands forward.

13. To sign "_____" use the "open five" hand, starting at the chin, move clockwise in front of the face, and end with a closed fist.

14. To sign "_____" use the "flat" hand, palm facing back, and push it over the shoulder.

15. To sign "_____" touch the tips of both "I" hands and pull them apart in a circular motion.

16. To sign "_____" place the index and middle fingers, in the shape of an inverted "V," onto the left "open" palm.

17. To sign "_____" circle the "flat" hand on the chest clockwise.

18. To sign "_____" place the fingertips of both hands on the chest and rock back and forth.

19. To sign "_____" use both "flat" hands, palms facing each other, and move hands straight down.

20. To sign "_____" place the "flat" hand at the temple.

21. To sign "_____" place the "S" hand at the temple and then snap open the index finger.

22. To sign "_____" move the "F" hands from each side of the mouth outward.

23. To sign "_____" twist "F" hands alternately back and forth several times, then add "person."

24. To sign "_____" rub the right "H" back and forth on top of the left "H" hand.

25. To sign "_____" pivot both "Y" hands several times.

Quiz Answers

Alphabet Quiz Answers

1. R	5. T	8. K
2. B	6. Y	9. F
3. I	7. D	10. H
4. P		

True/False Awareness Quiz Answers

Questions 1 through 9 are all True.
Question 10 is False—there are twenty-six letters in the English alphabet.
Just checking to see if you were snoozing!

Letter Form Quiz Answers

1. A E M N O S T are formed with a closed hand.
2. B C D F I K L R U V W X Y are formed in a vertical position.
3. G H are formed in a horizontal position.
4. P Q are formed pointing downward.

Sign Practice Quiz Answers

1. My, mine	10. Good	18. Animal
2. Name	11. Future	19. Person
3. School	12. Road	20. Know
4. Excuse	13. Beautiful	21. Understand
5. Applause	14. Past	22. Cat
6. Tan	15. Spaghetti	23. Interpreter
7. Milk	16. Stand	24. Train
8. Thank you	17. Please	25. Play
9. Learn		

Sign Language Games

ABC Game

Starting with the first letter of the alphabet, each person will fingerspell an item in the selected category. Each person will repeat all previous fingerspelled words before adding her own selection. No duplicating is allowed. The categories can be of your choosing —for example: food, clothing, animals, occupations, furniture, drinks, plants, books, movies, music/musical instruments, etc. The last person can choose the next category. This game can also be played with signs instead of fingerspelling each word or both signs and fingerspelling can be combined during the game.

Color Game

Sign or fingerspell as many items as you can in thirty seconds that are the color red, blue, green, yellow, orange, white, pink, purple, brown, or black. This game requires a larger acquisition of signs.

Facial Expression and Body Language Game

A narrator reads a children's story, such as *Goldilocks*, *The Three Little Pigs*, *Snow White*, or *Cinderella*. Friends, family members, or students act out the parts using facial expression, body language, mime, and gestures. Only limited sign is needed for this game.

Knock Knock Game

There is a knock on the door. The player opens an imaginary door, and using facial expression, body language, mime, and gesture only, she will attempt to convey the message on the index card. Write any of the following, plus whatever else you may want to invent, on an index card for each player.

Knock Knock, open the imaginary door:

- You find a very large box wrapped up in beautiful paper, but it is too big to bring it through the door.

- You find a puppy.

- You find a man delivering a vase with roses.

- You find something very disgusting and slimy.

- You find a bag of rubbish.

- You find one million dollars.

- You find a very heavy box.

- You find a family of raccoons.

- You find another door.

- You find an old friend.

- You find a pizza delivery.

- You find a full-length mirror.

- You find a tornado.

- You find a photographer snapping your picture.

- You find a shiny new _____.

Brown Bag Game

Place three to five items in a small brown paper bag. Then describe each item using signs, fingerspelling if needed for brand names, acting out using the item if applicable, facial expression, body language, mime, and gestures. A more advanced level of this game can be played by placing three to five items in a brown bag that have related importance to the player. The player will describe each item and why the item is important to her. Examples:

- A bag of beach sand might be an important memory from a fabulous vacation getaway

- A picture of a family member, a family animal, place, or thing

- A souvenir from high school, college, and so on

- A letter, a book, or a movie ticket

- Collectibles, a piece of jewelry, and so on

Sign Opposites Game

One person signs a sentence or a single sign and the other person signs the opposite. Examples:

- Up / Down

- Winter / Summer

- Start the car / Stop the car

- Open the door / Close the door

Household Game

A person will act out the function of a household object. The receivers give the sign or write out the name of the object. Examples:

- Unlocking a door: a key

- Washing dishes: dish liquid or a dishwasher

- Cleaning the floor: a broom, vacuum, or mop

Twins Game

Choose a category such as trees, food, clothing, animals, or colors. Players are set up in pairs. A signal to start is given, and both players simultaneously fingerspell or sign only one item from the selected category. If the players fingerspell or sign the same item, they receive a point. The team with the most points wins.

Resources

Deaf/Sign Language Resources

ADCO Hearing Products, Inc.
5661 South Curtice Street
Littleton, CO 80120
Voice/TTY: 303-794-3928 or 800-726-0851
www.adcohearing.com

ALDA, Inc.
1131 Lake Street #204
Oak Park, IL 60301
Voice/Fax: 877-907-1738
TTY: 708-358-0135
www.alda.org

Americans with Disabilities Act
United States Department of Justice
Civil Rights Division
Voice: 800-514-0301
TTY: 800-514-0383
www.usdoj.gov/crt/ada

AT&T Relay Center
Relay Center Access: 800-855-2881
800-682-8786
www.consumer.att.com/relay/tty/index.html

Clarion by Advanced Bionics
Corporate Headquarters
Advanced Bionics Corporation
12740 San Fernando Road
Sylmar, CA 91342
Voice: 661-362-1400 or 800-678-2575
TTY: 800-678-3575
www.cochlearimplant.com

CODA International, Inc.
P.O. Box 30715
Santa Barbara, CA 93130-0715
www.coda-international.org

Dawn Sign Press
6130 Nancy Ridge Drive
San Diego, CA 92121-3223
Voice/TTY: 858-625-0600
www.dawnsign.com

Deafness Research Foundation
Hearing Health Magazine
641 Lexington Avenue, 15th Floor
New York, NY 10022
Phone: 212-328-9480
Fax: 212-328-9484
www.drf.org

Families for Hands and Voices
P.O. Box 371926
Denver, CO 80237
303-300-9763 or 866-422-0422
www.handsandvoices.org

Gallaudet University
800 Florida Avenue NE
Washington, D.C. 20002
Voice/TTY: 202-651-5000
www.gallaudet.edu

Garlic Press
1312 Jeppesen Avenue
Eugene, OR 97401
541-345-0063
www.garlicpress.com

Harris Communications
15155 Technology Drive
Eden Prairie, MN 55344-2277
Voice: 800-825-6758
TTY: 800-825-9187
www.harriscomm.com

Hearing Loss Association of America
(formerly Self-Help for Hard of Hearing
People SHHH)
7910 Woodmont Avenue, Suite 1200
Bethesda, MD 20814
Voice: 301-657-2248
TTY: 301-657-2249
www.hearingloss.org

National Association of the Deaf
814 Thayer Avenue
Silver Spring, MD 20910-4500
Voice: 301-587-1788
TTY: 301-587-1789
www.nad.org

**National Education for Assistance Dogs
Services (NEADS) National Campus**
305 Redemption Rock Trail South
Princeton, MA 01541
Voice/TDD: 978-422-9064
www.neads.org

National Technical Institute for the Deaf
Lyndon Baines Johnson Building
52 Lomb Memorial Drive
Rochester, NY 14623-5604
Voice/TTY: 716-475-6700
www.rit.edu/NTID

National Theatre of the Deaf
139 North Main Street
W. Hartford, CT 06107
Voice: (860) 236-4193 or 800-300-5179
Relay: 866-327-8877
Video: 800-NTD-1967
www.ntd.org

Registry of Interpreters for the Deaf, Inc.
333 Commerce Street
Alexandria, VA 22314
Voice: 703-838-0030
TTY: 703-838-0459
www.rid.org

Sign Media, Inc.
4020 Blackburn Lane
Burtonsville, MD 20866-1167
Phone: 800-475-4756 or 301-421-0268
www.signmedia.com

Soundbytes
108 Industrial Drive
Jersey City, NJ 07305
Voice/TTY: 888-816-8191
www.soundbytes.com

Ultratec
450 Science Drive
Madison, WI 53711
Voice/TTY: 608-238-5400
www.ultratec.com

Websites

ASL Info
www.aslinfo.com/deafculture.cfm

ASL Pro
www.aslpro.com

American Sign Language Fonts
http://babel.uoregon.edu/yamada/fonts/asl.html

American Society for Deaf Children
www.deafchildren.org

ASL Dictionary
www.bconnex.net/~randys

Baby Sign Language
www.babysignlanguage.net
www.babies-and-sign-language.com
www.mybabycantalk.com
www.signingbaby.com

Clerc Center
http://clerccenter.gallaudet.edu

Deaf Education
www.deafed.net

Deaf Life
www.DeafTrivia.com
www.deaf.com

Deaf Net
www.deaf.net

Deaf Performing Arts Network
www.d-pan.com

DeafWeb Washington
www.deafweb.org/natlorgs.htm

Deaf Missions Official Online/Animated Dictionary of Religious Signs
www.deafmissions.com

Ear Surgery Information Center
www.earsurgery.org

Food and Drug Administration
www.fda.gov

Handspeak
www.handspeak.com

Hearing Health
www.hearinghealth.net

KODA
www.koda-info.org

Life Print
www.lifeprint.com

Michigan State University
http://commtechlab.msu.edu/sites/aslweb/browser.htm

National Association of the Deaf Information Center
www.nad.org/infocenter

Say What Club
www.saywhatclub.com

Signing Online
www.signingonline.com

Sorenson Communications
www.sorenson.com

Sign Language Books

A Basic Course in American Sign Language, by Carol Padden, Tom Humphries, and Terrence O'Rourke.

American Sign Language, "The Green Books," by Charlotte Baker-Shenk and Dennis Cokely.

American Sign Language: A Comprehensive Dictionary, by Martin L. A. Sternberg, EdD.

American Sign Language Medical Dictionary, by Elaine Costello.

American Sign Language Phrase Book, by Lou Fant.

American Sign Language the Easy Way, by David A. Stewart.

Conversational Sign Language II, by Willard Madsen.

Gallaudet Survival Guide to Signing, by Leonard G. Lane.

Handmade Alphabet, by Laura Rankin.

Learning American Sign Language, by Tom Humphries and Carol Padden.

Learn American Sign Language, by Arlene Rice (flashcards and booklet).

Medical Sign Language, by W. Joseph Garcia and Charles C. Thomas.

Random House Webster's American Sign Language Dictionary, by Elaine Costello, PhD.

Religious Signing, by Elaine Costello.

Signing Made Easy, by Rod R. Butterworth and Mickey Flodin.

Signs Across America, by Edgar H. Shroyer and Susan P. Shroyer.

Signs of the Times, by Edgar H. Shroyer.

Talking with Your Hands and Listening with Your Eyes, by Gabriel Grayson.

The Joy of Signing, by Lottie L. Riekehof.

The Joy of Signing Puzzle Book, by Linda Lascelle Hillebrand.

The Joy of Signing Puzzle Book 2, by Linda Lascelle Hillebrand with Lottie L. Riekehof.

The Perigee Visual Dictionary of Signing, by Rod R. Butterworth.

Cochlear Implant Information Resources

Children with Cochlear Implants in Educational Settings, by Mary Ellen Nevins and Patricia M. Chute.

Cochlear Implants: A Handbook, by Bonnie Poitras Tucker.

Cochlear Implants in Children, by John B. Christiansen and Irene W. Leigh.

Hear Again Back to Life, by Arlene Romoff.

The Handbook of Cochlear Implants and Children, by Nancy Tye-Murray.

The Handbook of Pediatric Audiology, by Sanford E. Gerber.

The Parent's Guide to Cochlear Implants, by Patricia M. chute and Mary Ellen Nevins.

Deaf Literature

A Deaf Adult Speaks Out, Third Edition, by Leo M. Jacobs.

A Loss for Words, by Lou Ann Walker.

A Man Without Words, by Susan Schaller.

American Deaf Culture: An Anthology, by Sherman Wilcox, ed.

Angels and Outcasts: An Anthology of Deaf Characters in Literature, by Trent Batson and Eugene Bergman, eds.

At Home among Strangers, by Jerome D. Schein.

Deaf History Unveiled, by John V. VanCleve, ed.

Deaf in America: Voices from a Culture, by Carol Padden and Tom Humphries.

Deaf Like Me, by Thomas S. Spradley and James P. Spradley.

Deaf President Now! The 1988 Revolution at Gallaudet University, by John B. Christiansen and Sharon N. Barnartt.

Everyone Here Spoke Sign Language: Hereditary Deafness on Martha's Vineyard, by Nora Ellen Groce.

I Have a Sister—My Sister Is Deaf, by Jeanne Whitehouse Peterson.

Mother Father Deaf: Living Between Sound and Silence, by Paul Michael Preston.

Seeing Voices, by Oliver Sacks.

The Mask of Benevolence: Disabling the Deaf Community, by Harlan Lane.

The Week the World Heard Gallaudet, by J. Gannon.

Train Go Sorry, by Leah Hager Cohen.

What's That Pig Outdoors? A Memoir of Deafness, by Henry Kisor.

When the Mind Hears: A History of the Deaf, by Harlan Lane.

You and Your Deaf Child, by John W. Adams.

Videos and CDs

These titles are easily available online, through any of the resources listed here, or in any of your favorite local bookstores or retailers where videos and multimedia entertainment materials are sold.

The American Sign Language Dictionary (CD-ROM)

American Sign Language Vocabulary (CD-ROM)

Baby See 'n Sign

Children of a Lesser God

Cochlear Implants: Covering the Basics

DEAFology 101: Deaf Culture as Seen Through the Eyes of a Deaf Humorist

From Mime to Sign

Sign with Your Baby

Signing Naturally

Sound and Fury

Glossary

acronym
A word formed from the first letters of several words.

active hand
The dominant hand; that is, the hand that moves when forming a sign.

ADA
Americans with Disabilities Act.

American Manual Alphabet
Twenty-six handshapes that represent the letters of the alphabet.

American Sign Language
A visual language that is the primary means of communication for the Deaf.

audiogram
A graph on which a hearing test result is recorded.

body shift
The movement of the signer's upper torso to represent two or more characters in a story or conversation.

The "Broken Ear"
The national symbol that represents deafness.

classifiers
A set of handshapes that represent categories, shapes, sizes, and movements of objects.

cochlear implant
A device surgically implanted into the skull to stimulate the auditory fibers, allowing certain amounts of hearing.

CODA
Acronym meaning "Children of Deaf Adults."

compound sign
Combining two or more signs.

Contact Sign

A form of communication that uses sign language in English word order and combines both elements of ASL and English. Also referred to as PSE (Pidgin Sign English).

cued speech

A set of eight handshapes used in four different locations around the face and mouth to help a lip reader distinguish between different sounds that look similar.

deaf

The term used to describe the condition in which the sense of hearing is nonfunctional for the purpose of everyday communication.

Deaf community

Deaf people who share common values, experiences, and a language.

decibel

A decibel, or dB, is a unit of measurement for the loudness of sound.

dominant hand

The strong, active hand that is used when signing.

fingerspelling

The application of the manual alphabet to spell out words in full or abbreviated form.

GA

The abbreviation for "go ahead" when typing on a TTY/TDD.

Gallaudet University

The only liberal arts college exclusively for the Deaf in the United States.

gesture

A body movement used in communicating.

grammar

The principles, structure, and rules of a language.

handshape

The shape of the hand, fingers, and palm when forming a sign.

iconic signs

Signs that resemble objects.

initialized signs

Signs that borrow letters from the manual alphabet.

interpreter
A person who translates spoken language into sign language and/or sign language into spoken language.

KODA
Acronym meaning "Kids of Deaf Adults."

lip reading
The ability to observe lip movement in order to understand oral language.

modified signs
Signs that have been changed, compressed, or altered.

nonmanual
Refers to signs that use head movement, facial expression, body language, and eye movement, and do not involve the hands.

OIC
The abbreviation for "Oh, I see" when typing on a TTY/TDD.

oralism
A method of communicating and educating a deaf person without the use of sign language.

postlingual deaf
Term used to describe a person whose deafness occurs after language is acquired.

prelingual deaf
Term used to describe a person whose deafness occurs at birth or before language is acquired.

PSE
Pidgin Sign English, a form of communication that uses sign language in English word order and combines both elements of ASL and English. Also referred to as Contact Sign.

Q
The abbreviation that is used when asking a question during a TTY/TDD conversation.

relay service
A service that provides a connection between a TTY user and a hearing person and uses a communication assistant, referred to as a CA.

sightline
The center of the signer's chest.

sign language

A manual language that uses symbols to represent ideas and concepts.

Signed English

A signing system that is used to represent spoken English.

signer

A person who uses Sign Language.

"Signer's Hands"

The national symbol representing Interpreters of Sign Language.

signing space

The signing space, which includes the sightline, is the area where the majority of the signs are formed.

sim-com/simultaneous communication

Manual and oral communication used simultaneously.

SK

The abbreviation for "stop keying" when typing on a TTY/TDD.

speech reading

The ability to observe lip movement in order to understand oral language.

synonym

A word that is different from but expresses the same meaning as another word.

syntax

The order in which words or signs are placed to form sentences and phrases.

timeline

An imaginary line through the body extending in front and behind.

total communication

The application of all methods of communicating.

TTY/TDD

A telecommunication device for the deaf that acts as a telephone.

variation

Differences in the formation and production of vocabulary.

Index

A

Abbreviations, 46, 48
Acronyms, 48
American Sign Language
    (ASL), 6, 9, 23-24
    defined, 2-3
Americans with Disabilities Act
    (ADA), 10, 117-18, 159
Animals, 160-67
Answering questions, 66
Apparel. *See* Clothing
ATM, 104

B

Baby sign language, 239-41, 244
    benefits of, 240
    recommended signs, 240-42
    for toddlers, 242
Bank, 104
Beethoven. *See* Van Beethoven,
    Ludwig
Bell, Alexander Graham, 191
Body language, 123, 254-55
Breakfast, 174-76
Broken ear symbol, 211-12

C

Calendar, 149-52
Capitalization, 48
Celebrations. *See* Holidays
Charades, 260
Child hearing health, 245-46
Children of deaf adults
    (CODAs), 10-11, 18

Classifiers, 127-33
    CL A, 128, 129
    CL B, 128, 130, 131-32
    CL C, 128, 129, 132
    CL 5, 128, 129, 132
    CL L, 128, 130, 132
    CL 1, 128, 129, 132
    CL 3, 128, 129
    three-finger, 232-33
Clerc, Laurent, 19
Clothing, 82-84
Cochlear Implant Education
    Center, 224
Cochlear implants, 223-24
College, 6, 56, 201-2
Color, 78-81
Communication in medical
    situations, 208-11
Compound signs, 140
Computers, 194-98
Connecticut Asylum at
    Hartford, 10
Contact signing, 4-5
Cued speech, 263

D

Dactylology, 128
Dalgarno, George, 128
Dance and sign language, 253-54
Days of the week, 150-52
Deaf community, 2, 23, 30, 75,
    218
Decibel
    defined, 220
    ranges, 220-21

De Bonnet, Juan Pablo, 41
De l'Epee, Abbé Charles
    Michel, 17-18
Dessert, 185-87
Dinner, 181-85
Direction, 234
    of hand, 34
Drama, 255-56

E

Ear, 217-18
Education, 19-20. *See also*
    School
    early and sign language,
        242-43
    jobs, 200-1
Educators, 9-10
    early, 11
Emotions, 87-89
Errors, 26
Etiquette, 58-59
Everyday chatter, 258-59
Explanations, 60
Expressions, 254-55
Eye contact, 31

F

Facial expressions, 120-22, 123
Family relationships, 110-14
Feelings. *See* Emotions
Fingerspelling, 5-6, 33-48
    accuracy, 34-35
    practice, 41-44
    situations for, 34

Food, 173-85
Fowler, Sophia, 18
Fractions, 103
Frelich, Phyllis, 251
Future, 144-45

G
Gallaudet,
    Thomas, 18-19
    College and University, 19-20,
        22-23, 139, 224, 263
Games for learning, 259-62
    charades, 260
    magic wand games, 261-62
Gender, 110

H
Hand
    to use, 26-29
    warm-up, 36
Handshape, 50-51, 56
Hearing aids, 221-22
Hearing health for children,
    245-46
Hearing loss
    defined, 218
    prevention, 219
    signs of, 219-20
Holidays, 155-56
Home, 190-92
    signs, 5
Hoy, William Ellsworth,
    141-42
Hubbard, Paul D., 139

I
Iconic sign, 246
Initialized signs, 44, 45
Interpreter, 8, 12

Interview, 70-75
    practice, 74-75
    questions, 75
Intonation, 57-58

J
Jordan, Dr. I. King, 23

L
Learning strategies, 30-31
Letters and numbers in
    conversations, 98
Loan signs, 44, 46
Location, 234
    of sign, 52-53, 56
Looks, description of, 85-86
Lunch, 176-90

M
Magic wand game, 261-62
Manual alphabet, 36-42
Manualism, 21
Martha's Vineyard, 16, 17
Matlin, Marlee, 22
McCallum, Heather
    Whitestone, 223. *See also*
    Whitestone, Heather
Medical
    communication, 208-11
    personnel, 12
    terms, 207-24
Milan Congress on Education
    for the Deaf, 20
Money, 104-7, 108
Months, 150
Movement, 136-38
    for sign, 53-54, 56
Music, 250-52
    religious songs, 252-53

rhythm, 251-52
translating lyrics, 251

N
Name sign, 74
Native system of sign language,
    16
Nature, 170-72
Number handshapes as
    descriptors, 97-98
Numbers, 94-103
    eleven through nineteen,
        98-100
    everyday, 108
    fractions, 103
    and letters in conversations,
        98
    to ninety, 100-2
    one hundred and up, 102-3
    one to ten, 94-97

O
Old French Sign Language
    (OFSL), 17
Oralism, 20-21

P
Palm position, 55, 56
Past, 144-45
People, 78
Person signs, 114-16
Pidgin Sign English (PSE), *See*
    Contact Signing
Plurals, 59-60
Possessives, 90-92
Practice routine, 181, 186, 254
Present, 144-45
Prevention of hearing loss, 219
Pronouns, 90

Public employees, 11
Punctuation, 201

Q
Questions, 63-76
  answering, 66
  interview, 75
  rhetorical, 76
  types of, 64
Quiz, 263-64

R
Relay service, 193
Rhetorical questions, 76
Role-playing, 123
Rules, 8, 49-61
  big four, 50-56

S
School, 75, 198-202
  college, 201-2
  subjects, 199-200
Seasons, 153-54
Service
  dogs, 158-60
  providers, 13
Sichard, Abbé Roche, 17-18
Sightline. *See* Signing space
Signed English (SE), 6, defined, 3-4
Signing space, 56-57
Sign language
  creators, 17-19
  defined, 1, 2
  as a language, 21-22
  origins of, 15-24
  users, 8-13
Sign order, 60-61
Sign variations, 69, 152, 226

Sign vocabulary, 7
Simplified signs, 246-47
Snacks, 180-81
Special-needs educators, 9
Sports, 138-40, 141-42
  compound signs, 140
States, 46-48
Stokoe, Dr.William C., 21-22
Storytelling, 123, 124-26

T
Telephone, 192-94
Three-finger classifier, 232-33
Time, 143-56
  calendar, 149-52
  general, 147-49
  holidays, 155-56
  past, present, future, 144-45
  seasons, 153-54
  specific, 146-47
Toddlers and sign language, 242
Total Communication (TC), 4, 262
Travel, 227-31. *See also* Vacation
TTY, 192-94

U
University. *See* College, Galladaut College/University
Usher's syndrome, 170

V
Vacation, 234-37
Van Beethoven, Ludwig, 250
Verbs, 124-26
Vineyard Sign Language, 16-17

W
Weather, 167-70
Weitbrecht, Robert H., 192
Whitestone, Heather, 21. *See also* McCallum, Heather Whitestone
Wh- word questions, 64, 66-68
Work, 203-6
Workplace, 117-18

Y
Yes-no questions, 65

Z
Zinser, Elizabeth Ann, 22-23

THE EVERYTHING SERIES!

BUSINESS & PERSONAL FINANCE

Everything® Accounting Book
Everything® Budgeting Book, 2nd Ed.
Everything® Business Planning Book
Everything® Coaching and Mentoring Book, 2nd Ed.
Everything® Fundraising Book
Everything® Get Out of Debt Book
Everything® Grant Writing Book, 2nd Ed.
Everything® Guide to Buying Foreclosures
Everything® Guide to Fundraising, $15.95
Everything® Guide to Mortgages
Everything® Guide to Personal Finance for Single Mothers
Everything® Home-Based Business Book, 2nd Ed.
Everything® Homebuying Book, 3rd Ed., $15.95
Everything® Homeselling Book, 2nd Ed.
Everything® Human Resource Management Book
Everything® Improve Your Credit Book
Everything® Investing Book, 2nd Ed.
Everything® Landlording Book
Everything® Leadership Book, 2nd Ed.
Everything® Managing People Book, 2nd Ed.
Everything® Negotiating Book
Everything® Online Auctions Book
Everything® Online Business Book
Everything® Personal Finance Book
Everything® Personal Finance in Your 20s & 30s Book, 2nd Ed.
Everything® Personal Finance in Your 40s & 50s Book, $15.95
Everything® Project Management Book, 2nd Ed.
Everything® Real Estate Investing Book
Everything® Retirement Planning Book
Everything® Robert's Rules Book, $7.95
Everything® Selling Book
Everything® Start Your Own Business Book, 2nd Ed.
Everything® Wills & Estate Planning Book

COOKING

Everything® Barbecue Cookbook
Everything® Bartender's Book, 2nd Ed., $9.95
Everything® Calorie Counting Cookbook
Everything® Cheese Book
Everything® Chinese Cookbook
Everything® Classic Recipes Book
Everything® Cocktail Parties & Drinks Book
Everything® College Cookbook
Everything® Cooking for Baby and Toddler Book
Everything® Diabetes Cookbook
Everything® Easy Gourmet Cookbook
Everything® Fondue Cookbook
Everything® Food Allergy Cookbook, $15.95
Everything® Fondue Party Book
Everything® Gluten-Free Cookbook
Everything® Glycemic Index Cookbook
Everything® Grilling Cookbook
Everything® Healthy Cooking for Parties Book, $15.95
Everything® Holiday Cookbook
Everything® Indian Cookbook
Everything® Lactose-Free Cookbook
Everything® Low-Cholesterol Cookbook

Everything® Low-Fat High-Flavor Cookbook, 2nd Ed., $15.95
Everything® Low-Salt Cookbook
Everything® Meals for a Month Cookbook
Everything® Meals on a Budget Cookbook
Everything® Mediterranean Cookbook
Everything® Mexican Cookbook
Everything® No Trans Fat Cookbook
Everything® One-Pot Cookbook, 2nd Ed., $15.95
Everything® Organic Cooking for Baby & Toddler Book, $15.95
Everything® Pizza Cookbook
Everything® Quick Meals Cookbook, 2nd Ed., $15.95
Everything® Slow Cooker Cookbook
Everything® Slow Cooking for a Crowd Cookbook
Everything® Soup Cookbook
Everything® Stir-Fry Cookbook
Everything® Sugar-Free Cookbook
Everything® Tapas and Small Plates Cookbook
Everything® Tex-Mex Cookbook
Everything® Thai Cookbook
Everything® Vegetarian Cookbook
Everything® Whole-Grain, High-Fiber Cookbook
Everything® Wild Game Cookbook
Everything® Wine Book, 2nd Ed.

GAMES

Everything® 15-Minute Sudoku Book, $9.95
Everything® 30-Minute Sudoku Book, $9.95
Everything® Bible Crosswords Book, $9.95
Everything® Blackjack Strategy Book
Everything® Brain Strain Book, $9.95
Everything® Bridge Book
Everything® Card Games Book
Everything® Card Tricks Book, $9.95
Everything® Casino Gambling Book, 2nd Ed.
Everything® Chess Basics Book
Everything® Christmas Crosswords Book, $9.95
Everything® Craps Strategy Book
Everything® Crossword and Puzzle Book
Everything® Crosswords and Puzzles for Quote Lovers Book, $9.95
Everything® Crossword Challenge Book
Everything® Crosswords for the Beach Book, $9.95
Everything® Cryptic Crosswords Book, $9.95
Everything® Cryptograms Book, $9.95
Everything® Easy Crosswords Book
Everything® Easy Kakuro Book, $9.95
Everything® Easy Large-Print Crosswords Book
Everything® Games Book, 2nd Ed.
Everything® Giant Book of Crosswords
Everything® Giant Sudoku Book, $9.95
Everything® Giant Word Search Book
Everything® Kakuro Challenge Book, $9.95
Everything® Large-Print Crossword Challenge Book
Everything® Large-Print Crosswords Book
Everything® Large-Print Travel Crosswords Book
Everything® Lateral Thinking Puzzles Book, $9.95
Everything® Literary Crosswords Book, $9.95
Everything® Mazes Book
Everything® Memory Booster Puzzles Book, $9.95

Everything® Movie Crosswords Book, $9.95
Everything® Music Crosswords Book, $9.95
Everything® Online Poker Book
Everything® Pencil Puzzles Book, $9.95
Everything® Poker Strategy Book
Everything® Pool & Billiards Book
Everything® Puzzles for Commuters Book, $9.95
Everything® Puzzles for Dog Lovers Book, $9.95
Everything® Sports Crosswords Book, $9.95
Everything® Test Your IQ Book, $9.95
Everything® Texas Hold 'Em Book, $9.95
Everything® Travel Crosswords Book, $9.95
Everything® Travel Mazes Book, $9.95
Everything® Travel Word Search Book, $9.95
Everything® TV Crosswords Book, $9.95
Everything® Word Games Challenge Book
Everything® Word Scramble Book
Everything® Word Search Book

HEALTH

Everything® Alzheimer's Book
Everything® Diabetes Book
Everything® First Aid Book, $9.95
Everything® Green Living Book
Everything® Health Guide to Addiction and Recovery
Everything® Health Guide to Adult Bipolar Disorder
Everything® Health Guide to Arthritis
Everything® Health Guide to Controlling Anxiety
Everything® Health Guide to Depression
Everything® Health Guide to Diabetes, 2nd Ed.
Everything® Health Guide to Fibromyalgia
Everything® Health Guide to Menopause, 2nd Ed.
Everything® Health Guide to Migraines
Everything® Health Guide to Multiple Sclerosis
Everything® Health Guide to OCD
Everything® Health Guide to PMS
Everything® Health Guide to Postpartum Care
Everything® Health Guide to Thyroid Disease
Everything® Hypnosis Book
Everything® Low Cholesterol Book
Everything® Menopause Book
Everything® Nutrition Book
Everything® Reflexology Book
Everything® Stress Management Book
Everything® Superfoods Book, $15.95

HISTORY

Everything® American Government Book
Everything® American History Book, 2nd Ed.
Everything® American Revolution Book, $15.95
Everything® Civil War Book
Everything® Freemasons Book
Everything® Irish History & Heritage Book
Everything® World War II Book, 2nd Ed.

HOBBIES

Everything® Candlemaking Book
Everything® Cartooning Book
Everything® Coin Collecting Book
Everything® Digital Photography Book, 2nd Ed.

Everything® Drawing Book
Everything® Family Tree Book, 2nd Ed.
Everything® Guide to Online Genealogy, $15.95
Everything® Knitting Book
Everything® Knots Book
Everything® Photography Book
Everything® Quilting Book
Everything® Sewing Book
Everything® Soapmaking Book, 2nd Ed.
Everything® Woodworking Book

HOME IMPROVEMENT

Everything® Feng Shui Book
Everything® Feng Shui Decluttering Book, $9.95
Everything® Fix-It Book
Everything® Green Living Book
Everything® Home Decorating Book
Everything® Home Storage Solutions Book
Everything® Homebuilding Book
Everything® Organize Your Home Book, 2nd Ed.

KIDS' BOOKS

All titles are $7.95
Everything® Fairy Tales Book, $14.95
Everything® Kids' Animal Puzzle & Activity Book
Everything® Kids' Astronomy Book
Everything® Kids' Baseball Book, 5th Ed.
Everything® Kids' Bible Trivia Book
Everything® Kids' Bugs Book
Everything® Kids' Cars and Trucks Puzzle and Activity Book
Everything® Kids' Christmas Puzzle & Activity Book
Everything® Kids' Connect the Dots
   Puzzle and Activity Book
Everything® Kids' Cookbook, 2nd Ed.
Everything® Kids' Crazy Puzzles Book
Everything® Kids' Dinosaurs Book
Everything® Kids' Dragons Puzzle and Activity Book
Everything® Kids' Environment Book $7.95
Everything® Kids' Fairies Puzzle and Activity Book
Everything® Kids' First Spanish Puzzle and Activity Book
Everything® Kids' Football Book
Everything® Kids' Geography Book
Everything® Kids' Gross Cookbook
Everything® Kids' Gross Hidden Pictures Book
Everything® Kids' Gross Jokes Book
Everything® Kids' Gross Mazes Book
Everything® Kids' Gross Puzzle & Activity Book
Everything® Kids' Halloween Puzzle & Activity Book
Everything® Kids' Hanukkah Puzzle and Activity Book
Everything® Kids' Hidden Pictures Book
Everything® Kids' Horses Book
Everything® Kids' Joke Book
Everything® Kids' Knock Knock Book
Everything® Kids' Learning French Book
Everything® Kids' Learning Spanish Book
Everything® Kids' Magical Science Experiments Book
Everything® Kids' Math Puzzles Book
Everything® Kids' Mazes Book
Everything® Kids' Money Book, 2nd Ed.
Everything® Kids' Mummies, Pharaoh's, and Pyramids
   Puzzle and Activity Book
Everything® Kids' Nature Book
Everything® Kids' Pirates Puzzle and Activity Book
Everything® Kids' Presidents Book
Everything® Kids' Princess Puzzle and Activity Book
Everything® Kids' Puzzle Book

Everything® Kids' Racecars Puzzle and Activity Book
Everything® Kids' Riddles & Brain Teasers Book
Everything® Kids' Science Experiments Book
Everything® Kids' Sharks Book
Everything® Kids' Soccer Book
Everything® Kids' Spelling Book
Everything® Kids' Spies Puzzle and Activity Book
Everything® Kids' States Book
Everything® Kids' Travel Activity Book
Everything® Kids' Word Search Puzzle and Activity Book

LANGUAGE

Everything® Conversational Japanese Book with CD, $19.95
Everything® French Grammar Book
Everything® French Phrase Book, $9.95
Everything® French Verb Book, $9.95
Everything® German Phrase Book, $9.95
Everything® German Practice Book with CD, $19.95
Everything® Inglés Book
Everything® Intermediate Spanish Book with CD, $19.95
Everything® Italian Phrase Book, $9.95
Everything® Italian Practice Book with CD, $19.95
Everything® Learning Brazilian Portuguese Book with CD, $19.95
Everything® Learning French Book with CD, 2nd Ed., $19.95
Everything® Learning German Book
Everything® Learning Italian Book
Everything® Learning Latin Book
Everything® Learning Russian Book with CD, $19.95
Everything® Learning Spanish Book
Everything® Learning Spanish Book with CD, 2nd Ed., $19.95
Everything® Russian Practice Book with CD, $19.95
Everything® Sign Language Book, $15.95
Everything® Spanish Grammar Book
Everything® Spanish Phrase Book, $9.95
Everything® Spanish Practice Book with CD, $19.95
Everything® Spanish Verb Book, $9.95
Everything® Speaking Mandarin Chinese Book with CD, $19.95

MUSIC

Everything® Bass Guitar Book with CD, $19.95
Everything® Drums Book with CD, $19.95
Everything® Guitar Book with CD, 2nd Ed., $19.95
Everything® Guitar Chords Book with CD, $19.95
Everything® Guitar Scales Book with CD, $19.95
Everything® Harmonica Book with CD, $15.95
Everything® Home Recording Book
Everything® Music Theory Book with CD, $19.95
Everything® Reading Music Book with CD, $19.95
Everything® Rock & Blues Guitar Book with CD, $19.95
Everything® Rock & Blues Piano Book with CD, $19.95
Everything® Rock Drums Book with CD, $19.95
Everything® Singing Book with CD, $19.95
Everything® Songwriting Book

NEW AGE

Everything® Astrology Book, 2nd Ed.
Everything® Birthday Personology Book
Everything® Celtic Wisdom Book, $15.95
Everything® Dreams Book, 2nd Ed.
Everything® Law of Attraction Book, $15.95
Everything® Love Signs Book, $9.95
Everything® Love Spells Book, $9.95
Everything® Palmistry Book
Everything® Psychic Book
Everything® Reiki Book

Everything® Sex Signs Book, $9.95
Everything® Spells & Charms Book, 2nd Ed.
Everything® Tarot Book, 2nd Ed.
Everything® Toltec Wisdom Book
Everything® Wicca & Witchcraft Book, 2nd Ed.

PARENTING

Everything® Baby Names Book, 2nd Ed.
Everything® Baby Shower Book, 2nd Ed.
Everything® Baby Sign Language Book with DVD
Everything® Baby's First Year Book
Everything® Birthing Book
Everything® Breastfeeding Book
Everything® Father-to-Be Book
Everything® Father's First Year Book
Everything® Get Ready for Baby Book, 2nd Ed.
Everything® Get Your Baby to Sleep Book, $9.95
Everything® Getting Pregnant Book
Everything® Guide to Pregnancy Over 35
Everything® Guide to Raising a One-Year-Old
Everything® Guide to Raising a Two-Year-Old
Everything® Guide to Raising Adolescent Boys
Everything® Guide to Raising Adolescent Girls
Everything® Mother's First Year Book
Everything® Parent's Guide to Childhood Illnesses
Everything® Parent's Guide to Children and Divorce
Everything® Parent's Guide to Children with ADD/ADHD
Everything® Parent's Guide to Children with Asperger's
   Syndrome
Everything® Parent's Guide to Children with Anxiety
Everything® Parent's Guide to Children with Asthma
Everything® Parent's Guide to Children with Autism
Everything® Parent's Guide to Children with Bipolar Disorder
Everything® Parent's Guide to Children with Depression
Everything® Parent's Guide to Children with Dyslexia
Everything® Parent's Guide to Children with Juvenile Diabetes
Everything® Parent's Guide to Children with OCD
Everything® Parent's Guide to Positive Discipline
Everything® Parent's Guide to Raising Boys
Everything® Parent's Guide to Raising Girls
Everything® Parent's Guide to Raising Siblings
Everything® Parent's Guide to Raising Your
   Adopted Child
Everything® Parent's Guide to Sensory Integration Disorder
Everything® Parent's Guide to Tantrums
Everything® Parent's Guide to the Strong-Willed Child
Everything® Parenting a Teenager Book
Everything® Potty Training Book, $9.95
Everything® Pregnancy Book, 3rd Ed.
Everything® Pregnancy Fitness Book
Everything® Pregnancy Nutrition Book
Everything® Pregnancy Organizer, 2nd Ed., $16.95
Everything® Toddler Activities Book
Everything® Toddler Book
Everything® Tween Book
Everything® Twins, Triplets, and More Book

PETS

Everything® Aquarium Book
Everything® Boxer Book
Everything® Cat Book, 2nd Ed.
Everything® Chihuahua Book
Everything® Cooking for Dogs Book
Everything® Dachshund Book
Everything® Dog Book, 2nd Ed.
Everything® Dog Grooming Book

Everything® Dog Obedience Book
Everything® Dog Owner's Organizer, $16.95
Everything® Dog Training and Tricks Book
Everything® German Shepherd Book
Everything® Golden Retriever Book
Everything® Horse Book, 2nd Ed., $15.95
Everything® Horse Care Book
Everything® Horseback Riding Book
Everything® Labrador Retriever Book
Everything® Poodle Book
Everything® Pug Book
Everything® Puppy Book
Everything® Small Dogs Book
Everything® Tropical Fish Book
Everything® Yorkshire Terrier Book

REFERENCE

Everything® American Presidents Book
Everything® Blogging Book
Everything® Build Your Vocabulary Book, $9.95
Everything® Car Care Book
Everything® Classical Mythology Book
Everything® Da Vinci Book
Everything® Einstein Book
Everything® Enneagram Book
Everything® Etiquette Book, 2nd Ed.
Everything® Family Christmas Book, $15.95
Everything® Guide to C. S. Lewis & Narnia
Everything® Guide to Divorce, 2nd Ed., $15.95
Everything® Guide to Edgar Allan Poe
Everything® Guide to Understanding Philosophy
Everything® Inventions and Patents Book
Everything® Jacqueline Kennedy Onassis Book
Everything® John F. Kennedy Book
Everything® Mafia Book
Everything® Martin Luther King Jr. Book
Everything® Pirates Book
Everything® Private Investigation Book
Everything® Psychology Book
Everything® Public Speaking Book, $9.95
Everything® Shakespeare Book, 2nd Ed.

RELIGION

Everything® Angels Book
Everything® Bible Book
Everything® Bible Study Book with CD, $19.95
Everything® Buddhism Book
Everything® Catholicism Book
Everything® Christianity Book
Everything® Gnostic Gospels Book
Everything® Hinduism Book, $15.95
Everything® History of the Bible Book
Everything® Jesus Book
Everything® Jewish History & Heritage Book
Everything® Judaism Book
Everything® Kabbalah Book
Everything® Koran Book
Everything® Mary Book
Everything® Mary Magdalene Book
Everything® Prayer Book

Everything® Saints Book, 2nd Ed.
Everything® Torah Book
Everything® Understanding Islam Book
Everything® Women of the Bible Book
Everything® World's Religions Book

SCHOOL & CAREERS

Everything® Career Tests Book
Everything® College Major Test Book
Everything® College Survival Book, 2nd Ed.
Everything® Cover Letter Book, 2nd Ed.
Everything® Filmmaking Book
Everything® Get-a-Job Book, 2nd Ed.
Everything® Guide to Being a Paralegal
Everything® Guide to Being a Personal Trainer
Everything® Guide to Being a Real Estate Agent
Everything® Guide to Being a Sales Rep
Everything® Guide to Being an Event Planner
Everything® Guide to Careers in Health Care
Everything® Guide to Careers in Law Enforcement
Everything® Guide to Government Jobs
Everything® Guide to Starting and Running a Catering
   Business
Everything® Guide to Starting and Running a Restaurant
**Everything® Guide to Starting and Running
   a Retail Store**
Everything® Job Interview Book, 2nd Ed.
Everything® New Nurse Book
Everything® New Teacher Book
Everything® Paying for College Book
Everything® Practice Interview Book
Everything® Resume Book, 3rd Ed.
Everything® Study Book

SELF-HELP

Everything® Body Language Book
Everything® Dating Book, 2nd Ed.
Everything® Great Sex Book
**Everything® Guide to Caring for Aging Parents,
   $15.95**
Everything® Self-Esteem Book
Everything® Self-Hypnosis Book, $9.95
Everything® Tantric Sex Book

SPORTS & FITNESS

Everything® Easy Fitness Book
Everything® Fishing Book
Everything® Guide to Weight Training, $15.95
Everything® Krav Maga for Fitness Book
Everything® Running Book, 2nd Ed.
Everything® Triathlon Training Book, $15.95

TRAVEL

Everything® Family Guide to Coastal Florida
Everything® Family Guide to Cruise Vacations
Everything® Family Guide to Hawaii
Everything® Family Guide to Las Vegas, 2nd Ed.
Everything® Family Guide to Mexico
Everything® Family Guide to New England, 2nd Ed.

Everything® Family Guide to New York City, 3rd Ed.
**Everything® Family Guide to Northern California
   and Lake Tahoe**
Everything® Family Guide to RV Travel & Campgrounds
Everything® Family Guide to the Caribbean
Everything® Family Guide to the Disneyland® Resort, California
   Adventure®, Universal Studios®, and the Anaheim
   Area, 2nd Ed.
Everything® Family Guide to the Walt Disney World Resort®,
   Universal Studios®, and Greater Orlando, 5th Ed.
Everything® Family Guide to Timeshares
Everything® Family Guide to Washington D.C., 2nd Ed.

WEDDINGS

Everything® Bachelorette Party Book, $9.95
Everything® Bridesmaid Book, $9.95
Everything® Destination Wedding Book
Everything® Father of the Bride Book, $9.95
Everything® Green Wedding Book, $15.95
Everything® Groom Book, $9.95
Everything® Jewish Wedding Book, 2nd Ed., $15.95
Everything® Mother of the Bride Book, $9.95
Everything® Outdoor Wedding Book
Everything® Wedding Book, 3rd Ed.
Everything® Wedding Checklist, $9.95
Everything® Wedding Etiquette Book, $9.95
Everything® Wedding Organizer, 2nd Ed., $16.95
Everything® Wedding Shower Book, $9.95
Everything® Wedding Vows Book, 3rd Ed., $9.95
Everything® Wedding Workout Book
Everything® Weddings on a Budget Book, 2nd Ed., $9.95

WRITING

Everything® Creative Writing Book
Everything® Get Published Book, 2nd Ed.
Everything® Grammar and Style Book, 2nd Ed.
Everything® Guide to Magazine Writing
Everything® Guide to Writing a Book Proposal
Everything® Guide to Writing a Novel
Everything® Guide to Writing Children's Books
Everything® Guide to Writing Copy
Everything® Guide to Writing Graphic Novels
Everything® Guide to Writing Research Papers
Everything® Guide to Writing a Romance Novel, $15.95
Everything® Improve Your Writing Book, 2nd Ed.
Everything® Writing Poetry Book